PRAGUE
CHURCHES AND TEMPLES

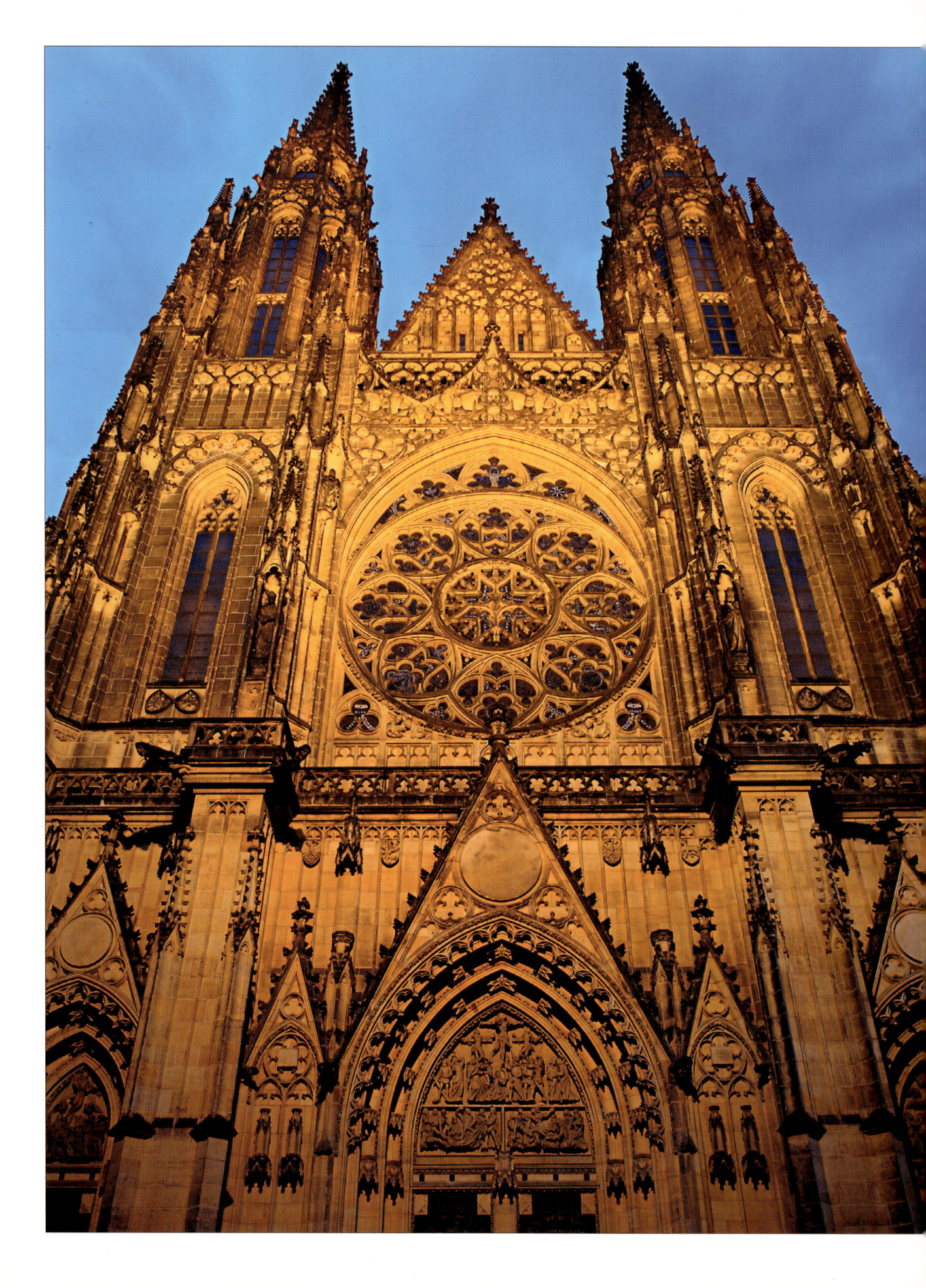

PRAGUE
CHURCHES AND TEMPLES

TOMÁŠ VUČKA

slovart

© 2013 Slovart Publishing house
Text copyright © 2013 Tomáš Vučka
Photography © 2013 Roman Maleček, Jan Rendek, Zdeněk Thoma
Translation © 2013 Jerzy Cieslar

Translated from Czech by Jerzy Cieslar
Edited by Ryan Kelley
Issued by Slovart Publishing house in Prague, 2013
Responsible editor Jan Heller
Graphic layout Branislav Gajdoš
Production Dana Klimová
Printed by Graspo CZ, Zlín

ISBN 978-80-7391-800-2
10 9 8 7 6 5 4 3 2 1

TABLE OF CONTENTS

6	Prague - Birth of a City on the Vltava
11	The Cathedral of St. Vitus, Wenceslas and Vojtěch
19	St. George's Basilica
23	Loretta
29	The Church of St. Peter and St. Paul at Vyšehrad
37	The Rotunda of St. Martin
41	The Church of the Virgin Mary under the Chain, Lesser Town
45	The Church of Our Lady of Victory
51	The Church of Our Lady before Týn
61	The Church of St. Hastal
65	The Church of St. Havel
71	Bethlehem Chapel
75	St. Martin in the Wall Church
79	The Church of St. Jiljí
87	The Church of Our Lady of the Snow, New Town
91	The Church of St. Henry and Kunhuta
95	The Church of the Holy Ghost
101	The Church of St. Peter
109	The Church of St. Steven
113	St. Longin's Rotunda
117	The Church of St. Cyril and Methodius
121	The Church of the Most Sacred Heart of Our Lord
125	Old New Synagogue
129	Spanish Synagogue
133	Maisel Synagogue
136	... Finally, a few more steps through Prague

PRAGUE
A CITY IS BORN ON THE VLTAVA

It's a city wedged between small hills, blown by the soft wind sweeping from the dark green surface of the Vltava; a city which back in 1518 already boasted the proud postscript *caput regni* and later *mater urbium;* a city called "hundred-spired" and "magical", which in its hundreds of years of dramatic development has been shrouded in secrets and mystery, one of which is its own name, Prague. Perhaps we can believe the ancient prophesy of the princess Libuse, who saw in her visions the beauty and nobility of a future city along the Vltava, a city whose "fame will touch the stars"; perhaps we can believe her words that somewhere down along the river an unknown man was even then hewing the threshold of his home, and in accordance with this threshold (*prah*) a future city would be named... Or perhaps we can take a more practical view and derive the name of this old Slavic city from the shallow waters washing on the riverbanks near the place where the Czech King and Roman Emperor Charles IV would build his great bridge. Or furthermore, perhaps the name of the city was taken from the small, stony, parched hill, the promontory above the Vltava, where the first governmental city established its fortified settlement, where St. George's Basilica was later built, where the heights of the thin Gothic tower of St. Vitus cathedral would later extend, and across which the palace of Prague castle would later expand.

In prehistoric times a whole range of various tribes resided within the territories of what is known today as Prague. It is possible to consider the settlement of what is known as the Linear Pottery culture as the oldest, which dates back to seven thousand years ago. Later, the Germans and Celts also passed through the Prague basin. The Slavs probably started to settle here around the sixth century AD, and by the ninth century the tall, desolate, rugged promontory above the Vltava had already become a key location. Přemysl's fortified settlement arose there, inside of which Duke Bořivoj built the second Christian church on Czech lands, which was dedicated to the Virgin Mary. When his son, Spytihněv I, sat on the Duke's throne at the beginning of the tenth century, he replaced the primitive fencing with a massive bank with protective spires. In addition, the Duke's palace was also expanded, to become more comfortable. The foundation for the future Prague castle, the seat of the Czech King and later the president, was also put in place. From this small hill, the Přemyslids began to rule the valleys and basins along the banks of the Vltava, where from the original outdoor settlement a medieval city began to grow, and slowly but surely the capital city, a royal city, the center of the Czech lands, began to come into being.

The hilly landscape under the castle, sharply sloping downward to the river, was already a permanent settlement in the tenth century; it stretched from the right bank of the Vltava, opposite the Hradčany promontory, and over to the Vyšehrad cliffs to today's Peter quarter. The original country settlement changed relatively quickly and took on the character of a city. Back in the tenth century, Ibrahim ibn Jacob, the Arab trader in the services of the Córdoban caliph Abd ar-Rahmán III, described the Prague settlement as a predominantly stone city, which underlined its significance and emphasized its big and rapid expansion. In the years 1232-1234 the settlement in the bend of the Vltava river - Old Town (*Antiqua civitas Pragensis*), also formerly called Greater Town or Prague town - acquired the status of an urban municipality, and in year 1257 Prague's modern-day Lesser Town was also promoted to city status by Přemysl Otakar II, in contrast to the city's former name of Small Town.

The Jewish ghetto, or Jewish quarter, was also part of Old Town (*Judenstadt*), which was called *Josefov* starting in 1850. Jewish people were already settled in the Prague river basin back in the tenth century; at first, they settled in the area of today's Lesser Town, but at the beginning of the twelfth century they relocated to the area now called Old Town. The Jews lived in this labyrinth of mostly unpaved, narrow streets until 1215, when the Fourth Lateran Council labeled them as culprits directly responsible for the death of Christ and handed them a centuries-long prison sentence. The ghetto, separated from the Christian part of Old Town up until 1781 when Josef II issued his Tolerance patent, became firmly attached to Jewish identity in the city, and the symbolic borders themselves remained basically unchanged. As a result of this, it became necessary to utilize every piece of available space: every corner was built up, houses acquired bizarre extensions, and in the space-limited Jewish cemetery people were buried in many layers placed on top of each other... unfortunately, this meant that because of floods from the Vltava, the cemetery was repeatedly washed out, along with the remains of deceased people. The Jewish ghetto was narrowed from time to time in cruel pogroms, and in the end grew into the form of a dusky labyrinth with narrow, winding little streets and courtyards. Only in 1884 were the Jewish inhabitants allowed to move to other Prague quarters.

Old Town didn't just hide a Jewish ghetto in its heart; Havel town also arose inside of it. Havel town is an area built around the Church of St. Havel (Gallus), which originated from an initiative of Wenceslas I. Havel town (*Civitas circa St. Gallum*), a de facto city inside a city, inhabited mostly by German artisans and built at the southern edge of Old Town, paved the way, in the year 1348, for the founding of New Town, the grandiose urban project of Charles IV.

The developed area on the right bank of the Vltava, from the fortification wall in the area of today's Na Příkopech street over to Charles Square, reaching almost to Vyšehrad, was dramatically expanded by these initiatives. At the same time, the first narrow streets of this new quarter also slowly started climbing up the hill of the future Vinohrady. The separate urban areas, that is Hradčany, Lesser Town, Old Town, and New Town, were later unified in 1784 into *the Royal Capital City of Prague*. At that time, Emperor Joseph II began to implement his reforms which, in the spirit of the Enlightenment, subjected the existence of churches, monasteries and the religious order to the condition of their practical, functional usage. On the basis of these reforms, there were a whole range of very old, architecturally, historically and artistically valuable religious buildings which were demolished, or, in the best case, transformed into military bases or warehouses for military provisions.

On the cusp of the 19th century, the original countryside settlements around the royal city of Prague quickly started to change character. The countryside homesteads and farms began to give way to manufacturing centers, propelled by the Industrial Revolution. During the course of the nineteenth century this tendency swung into full gear, and the idyllic landscape in close proximity to the *Royal city of Prague*, which some Prague residents visited for trips and the more ambitious for summer flats, gradually transformed into an industrial location; the future city periphery became interspersed with factory halls, worker colonies, and new, ever-expanding blocks of flats. During these busy years, Smíchov, an area located on the left side of the Vltava behind the original Újezd gate, became a typical example of the working class neighborhoods which became the industrial heart of Prague; the same as happened in Karlín and later Libeň on the right bank or up the hill rising to Žižkov. It was only a matter of time until they would become more integrated with the greater Prague.

The oldest part of Prague wasn't immune to change either. With the equalization of the Jewish people and the opening of their ghetto, a question was presented to the urban dwellers: how to deal with the hygienically unsuitable conditions, and in many ways still medieval atmosphere, prevalent in the Jewish city. In 1893 the rehabilitation of Old Town was initiated, controversial even to this day, and the ghetto was flattened to the ground. In its place grew modern, Gothic-style apartment buildings, while narrow and crooked alleyways were replaced by wide, straight avenues, betraying their inspiration in the vast boulevards of modern Paris. Fortunately, at least a few original buildings were able to escape that sad fate, primarily the Jewish cemetery and some synagogues. Along with the revitalization of the Jewish ghetto, the regulation of the Vltava also took place, whose flooding often had catastrophic consequences for Prague. This regulation consisted primarily of the construction of a massive stone embankment, which in the case of Old Town led to the original street level in some places being raised by several meters. With the regulation of the Vltava came the demise of another quarter, the original settlements under Vyšehrad, called Podskalí. This peculiar area on the Vltava began to disappear in 1876, the last homes being destroyed in 1924. From the original Podskalí, only the Podskalí Custom's Office remains, a small house on the Výtoň...

At the end of the nineteenth century, there was more and more discussion about connecting Royal Prague with the quickly developing industrial area, still independent at that time. It primarily concerned Smíchov, Karlín, Libeň and Žižkov. Efforts for connecting these areas with Prague foundered on unrealistic expectations and all kinds of quarrels; the areas in question wanted to become part of Prague, but nevertheless they also demanded to retain their privileges and autonomy. Therefore, attempts connecting Karlín, Žižkov, Královské Vinohrady and Smíchov were shipwrecked again and again. The first area to be connected with Prague was Libeň, which became *Greater Prague* and joined the royal city in 1901. Further negotiations were disrupted by World War I. Nevertheless, after its conclusion and within the mist of the euphoria surrounding the birth of an independent Czechoslovakia, visions of the future form of Prague began to be seen in a new light. On the basis of a motion of the National Assembly in November 1918, Greater Prague came into being on the first of January in 1922, in which Karlín, Vysočany, Smíchov, Bubeneč, Dejvice, Košíře, Žižkov, Vinohrady, Vršovice, Nusle, and Podolí were finally included.

In the following decades, Prague went through additional transformations, unfortunately often of a more harmful nature. As far back as in the 1950's, the urgent necessity to deal with the ever increasing lack of apartments became a reality, which led to the gradual construction of blocks of flats. These were initially built within the scope of the older quarters (Žižkov, Vršovice), then later - primarily starting in the 1970's - in a gigantic agglomeration of blocks of flats, surrounding Prague. However, the Social realist architecture unfortunately made its way into the historical center of the city as well, and from undeveloped vacant lots grew glass and concrete constructions, whose design disturbs the area's original architectonic character. The most lamented blow to the center of Prague occurred through the lengthening of the Prague arterial road, which also completely destroyed the area in front of the main railway station (Wilson); this also included the upper end of Wenceslas Square with the National Museum building. Prague has experienced another building boom since the 1990's, where vast, worn out factory complexes in Karlín, Vysočany and Smíchov have been making way for new apartment and office buildings. In some cases the changes are for the best, but through insensitive intervention in many cases, the old individual character of these past proletarian quarters of the Prague periphery has been erased.

Prague has gone through many dramatic events in its centuries-long history. Many valuable architectural historical sites were destroyed during the hardships of war, others through waves of religious and ideological fanaticism. It was therefore great luck for Prague that it basically escaped bombardment during World War II, and didn't have to meet the fate of British Coventry, or the fate of many cities in France and especially Germany. Socialist realism left many welts in Prague, whether through poorly thought out construction or disinterest in the maintenance of historical sites. In spite of all this, however, Prague as a whole remains a work of art, a living artistic and architectural gallery. Its churches and chapels, temples, rotundas and synagogues are a unique testament to its historical, artistic, cultural, and primarily its spiritual crystallization.

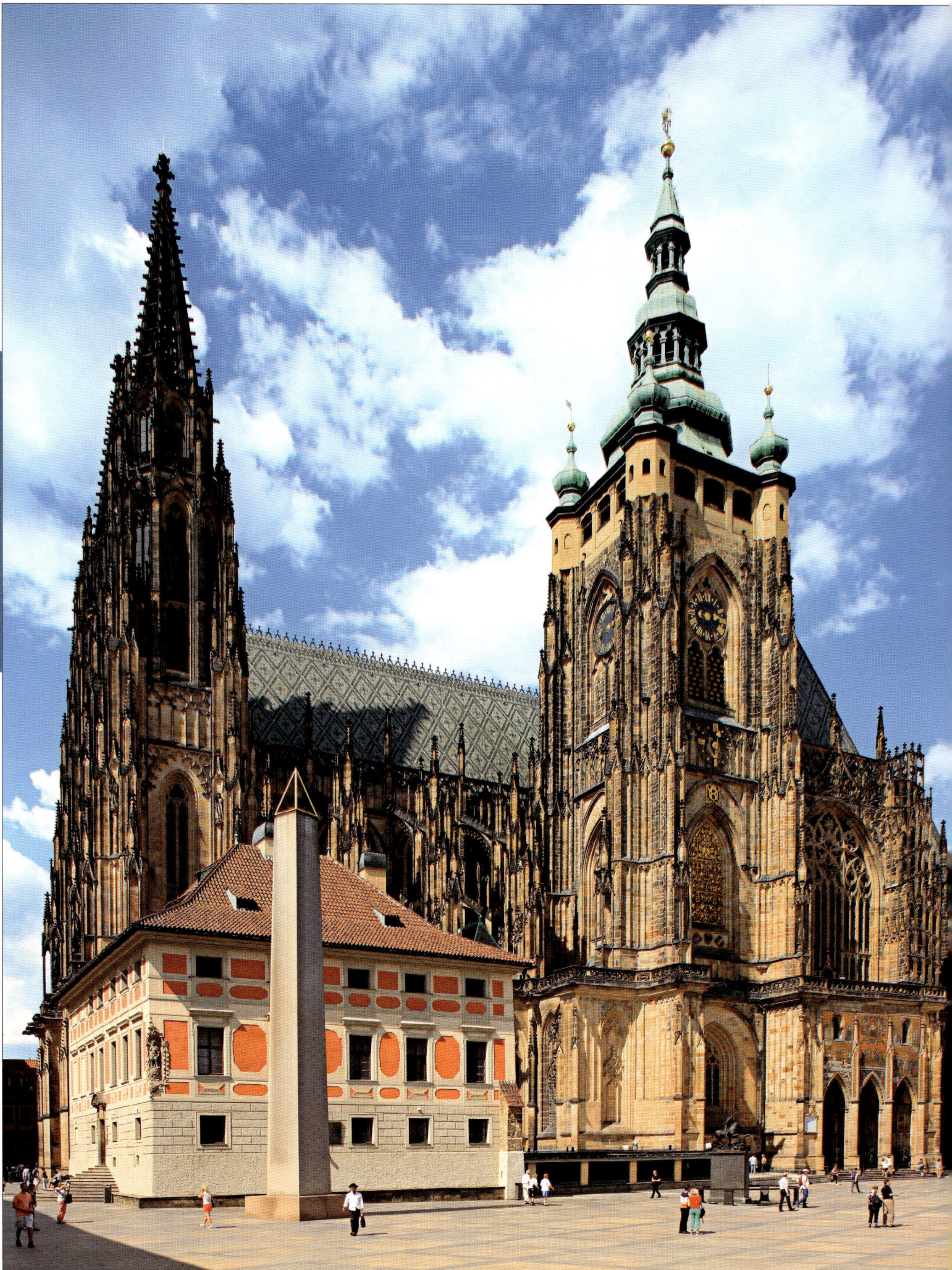

THE CATHEDRAL OF ST. VITUS, WENCESLAS AND VOJTĚCH

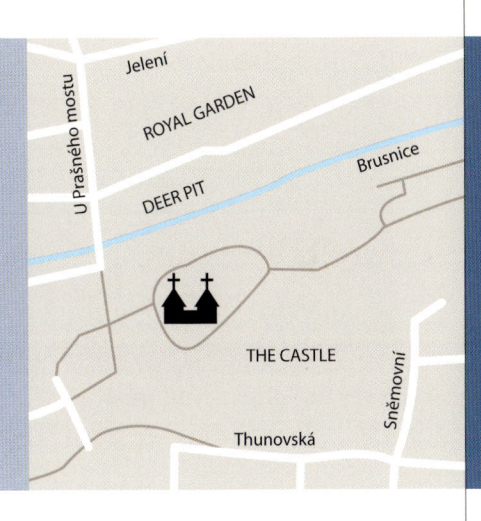

The three-aisle Gothic cathedral of St. Vitus, Wenceslas and Vojtěch at Prague Castle, the main church of the Archbishop of Prague and the place of coronation as well as the final resting place of the Czech King, has been a dominant feature of Prague for centuries.

Castle, Prague 1 - Hradčany
Transport: Tram 1, 18, 22, 25 Prague Castle
Worship:
Mon-Fri 7:00 am, Fri 6:00 pm, Sat 7:00 am,
Sun 8:30 am, 10:00 am, 5:00 pm

1344-1419 1st phase of construction
1490-1510 2nd phase of construction
1556-1593 3rd phase of construction
1873-1929 Extension of the western part of the cathedral

On the rocky promontory where Prague Castle stands today, a fort had already been built back in the ninth century. Duke Bořivoj had a church built inside of it, which was dedicated to the Virgin Mary. His son, Spytihněv I, subsequently began with the construction of a separate Přemyslid fortified settlement. When Vratislav I sat on the throne, the settlement gained another church around 915, dedicated to St. George, which became the duke's central temple. Between 926 and 929 a third sanctuary arose inside the fortified settlement, beginning a long chapter in the future of St. Vitus Cathedral. The new church was built by Prince Duke Wenceslas, who would later become the canonized patron saint of the Czech lands. The church had the shape of a relatively large rotunda with four apses, oriented by crosses facing the four worldly directions. The rotunda was dedicated to St. Vitus, whose relic - the remains of his arm - was obtained by Duke Wenceslas, as a gift from the French king, Jindřich I., called the Bird Catcher.

In 935, Duke Wenceslas was murdered by his brother Boleslaus and his remains were placed under the southern apse of the rotunda. The grave of St. Wenceslas became a place of worship and the spiritual focal point of Prague Castle, and is there in its original place to this day. The foundation of the southern apse of the original rotunda also sur-

Prague Castle with St. Vitus Cathedral, view from Strahov

vived, along with the grave of Wenceslas, above which later arose St. Wenceslas's chapel. By disposition of the Prague diocese in 973, it gained a new function as the new spiritual center of the Czech lands. St. Vitus and St. Wenceslas are already mentioned as churches in the founding documents of the diocese, and the name of St. Vojtěch was also added in 1039, when Duke Břetislav I. placed the remains of St. Vojtěch under the western apse. In spite of its rather large size, the rotunda soon ceased to suffice. Therefore, around 1060, Spytihněv II began building a larger temple, which was erected on the site of the rotunda in the form of a three-aisle basilica with a transverse aisle on the western side. The dedication to St. Vitus, Wenceslas and Vojtěch was also passed on to this new building. The basilica, which was almost destroyed before completion by a massive fire in 1090, in the end attained respectable dimensions: seventy meters long, and over thirty meters wide. It was completed in 1096.

With the accession of John of Bohemia to the Czech throne, another chapter in the history of St. Vitus cathedral began. Charles IV, at that time only the Moravian margrave, enchanted by French Gothic architecture, was initiating the construction of a new temple, which would grow into a representative, majestic cathedral on a global architectural and artistic level. Its building was closely connected to the promotion of the Prague diocese to the archdiocese on the 30th of April, 1344. The first Prague archbishop, Arnost of Pardubice, a close friend of Charles IV, thereby gained the right to crown Czech kings. Approximately six months later, exactly on the 21st of November 1344, King John of Bohemia, his sons Charles and Jan Jindřich, and the Prague archbishop laid the founding stone for the future cathedral. Matthias of Arras, summoned to Prague from Avignon, became its chief builder.

The construction, which was influenced by French cathedrals, commenced with the presbytery and chancel; eight chapels rose in a horseshoe-shaped ground plan, rising to the height of the gallery above the tall ground-floor windows. However, in 1352, Matthias from Arras, already an old man by that time, passed away. The builder Jindřich

Prague Castle with St. Vitus Cathedral

Parléř should have taken his place; however, on account of his age, he had to refuse the job. In his place he recommended his son, a young man named Petr, so that he would not be idle, and in 1356 Petr came to Prague. In spite of his youth, Petr Parléř proved himself capable in the function of *magister operis*, that is to say master architect. He was also responsible for the operation of the whole building's ironworks, and soon became a wealthy and respectable Prague townsman, later even becoming town councilor. He later brought his wife from Germany and settled permanently in Prague.

Under Parléř's leadership, construction advanced quickly. Around 1366, St. Vaclav's chapel was completed, which Parléř adorned with a unique, star-shaped vault. Above it, Parléř built a crowning chamber, where the jewels of the Czech crown were kept, and still are to this day. Next to St. Wenceslas chapel, a southern wall of the future transverse aisle came into being, tall and with a Gothic arch; it was only in 1909 that a great, richly adorned neo-Gothic window was fitted. Under the space in the wall of the unfinished transverse aisle, on the golden gate which was at the same level, a mosaic based on the Final Judgment could be seen from 1371 onwards. Its author is unknown but is thought to be from a Venetian master, because the mosaic was made after the second coronation trip of Charles IV to Italy. As the construction of the cathedral continued, the original Spytihněv basilica was gradually demolished and the remains of the ruler were transferred to a sarcophagus inside the new Cathedral chapel. A final resting place in the unfinished temple was also made for Charles IV, who passed away in 1378. At that time, work had already begun on the arching of the cathedral, which was finished in 1385. The consecration of the cathedral was performed by Jan from Jenštejn and the temple was dedicated to St. Vitus and the Virgin Mary. Parléř's metal work also erected Vekou Tower at the southern wall of the unfinished aisle wall, later called Hassenburg Tower after the remains of the Archbishop Zajíce from Hassenburg, which are laid there. The tower was built to a height of around fifty meters; however, credit for it goes to Parléř's sons Jan and Václav. The

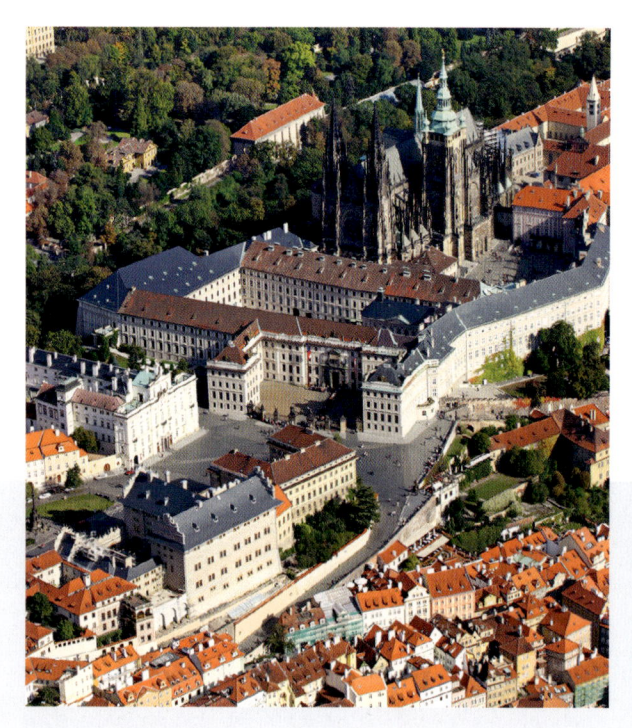

Hradčanské Square, The new royal palace, 1st and 2nd courtyard of Prague Castle

The Cathedral of St. Vitus, a view of the main nave

▶ The Cathedral of St. Vitus, chancel with the mausoleum of the Habsburgs

somewhat heavier architectural signature of Matthias from Arras was replaced by the lightness founded upon a gentle, decorative ornamentation and a monumental system of supportive pillars. This created a strange ruggedness, which through the final impression of the massiveness of the cathedral walls transforms into fragility and delicacy.

Further work on the cathedral was interrupted by the Hussite wars. The metalwork was finished in 1419 and Parléř's sons prudently left Prague. The temple, actually only the unfinished torso, was at that time generously equipped with more than sixty altars. Two years after the departure of the Parléř sons, the Hussittes plundered the sanctuary, and in the following years, the destroyed cathedral remained abandoned. A giant hole in the unfinished southern transverse aisle wall, prepared for the magnificent and impressive Gothic window, was a reminder of the long-ago dream of King Charles the IV. That dream slowly started to come true with the accession of Vladislaus Jagellon to the Czech throne. In 1485, Vladislaus relocated his residence to Prague Castle, at that time falling into significant disrepair. A German builder, Benedict Ried, was called upon for its rejuvenation. He also had to simultaneously work on completing the destroyed cathedrals, so he only managed to lay the second foundation of the northern tower, facing the raised Hassenburg tower. Work on the cathedral was once again halted at that stage.

Charles' temple seemed to be under an inauspicious fate. In 1541, a massive fire spread in Lesser Town and Hradčany and the cathedral burned down. The only positive thing was the fact that the Parléř-built vault survived the giant fire and didn't collapse inwards. Even so, the repair of the temple took an unbelievably long time, all the way up to 1586. At that time, the builders Bonifác Wohlmut and Hans Tirol placed a Renaissance dome in the Hassenburg tower, under which the gallery was lifted, which survives even today. The short periods during which the cathedral was modified and repaired were again replaced by moments of destruction. When Friedrich von der Pfalz, the so-called Winter King, had been sitting on the Czech throne for merely a year, his fanatical pastor Abraham

15

1st courtyard of Prague Castle, the New Royal Palace and Cathedral of St. Vitus

Skultety smashed into the temple and carried out his anti-art campaign, destroying much of the furniture within. Better times for the temple had to wait until 1621 when, within the framework of re-Catholicization, the cathedral was transferred into the property of the Roman Catholic Church. Repairs were begun, but work was again interrupted by the Thirty Years War. Another attempt at its completion was triggered by the Turkish threat in Europe. Emperor Leopold I began to be interested in the possibility of completing the construction of cathedrals in approximately 1673. We can only guess at his motivation; to what extent his love for art and architecture played a role, and to what extent this attempt was prompted by the prophecy that declared that "he who finishes building the cathedrals will drive the Muslims out of Europe". In the end, the war with Turkey suppressed these meritorious intentions yet again.

The nineteenth century, with its nostalgic and romantic fondness for neo-Gothic aesthetics, ushered in a genuinely systematic and eventually fruit-bearing endeavor to complete the building of St. Vitus cathedral in a dignified manner. In 1861, an architect named Josef Kranner was named as head of the construction of the temple; by 1867, he had managed to reconstruct the most damaged parts of the temple. The following year, he submitted a project for the completion of the cathedral, in which he proposed building a north tower facing Hasenburg Tower; he planned to remove the Baroque dome in the tower and install a neo-Gothic style roof instead. However, in the end nothing came of these plans.

After the death of Kranner, construction was taken over by Josef Mocker. He abandoned the northern tower from Kranner's project and in its place built a pair of tall, thin towers into the façade of the three aisles, which were completed in 1892. However, even Mocker didn't live to see the completion of the cathedral, and after his death the work on the temple was entrusted to the young architect Kamil Hilbert. Hilbert restored Hassenburg Tower, on which the Baroque dome remained. He placed a massive window tracery in the empty space in the southern side of the trans-

View from St. George's Monastery

▼ St. Vitus Cathedral, the main façade

verse aisle, completed the vault in the finished aisles, and in 1910 he repaired St. Wenceslas' chapel. A unique discovery was made during its restoration: under the floor of the chapel were hidden the remains of the original rotunda with the saint's grave, along with parts of Spytihněv's basilica. In 1915, a large rosette window in the façade of the cathedral was completed. Work on the temple was finally finished in 1926. In May of 1929, the cathedral was consecrated, and in September of the same year, on the day of the thousand-year anniversary of St. Wenceslas's death, the cathedral was completed and handed over for use.

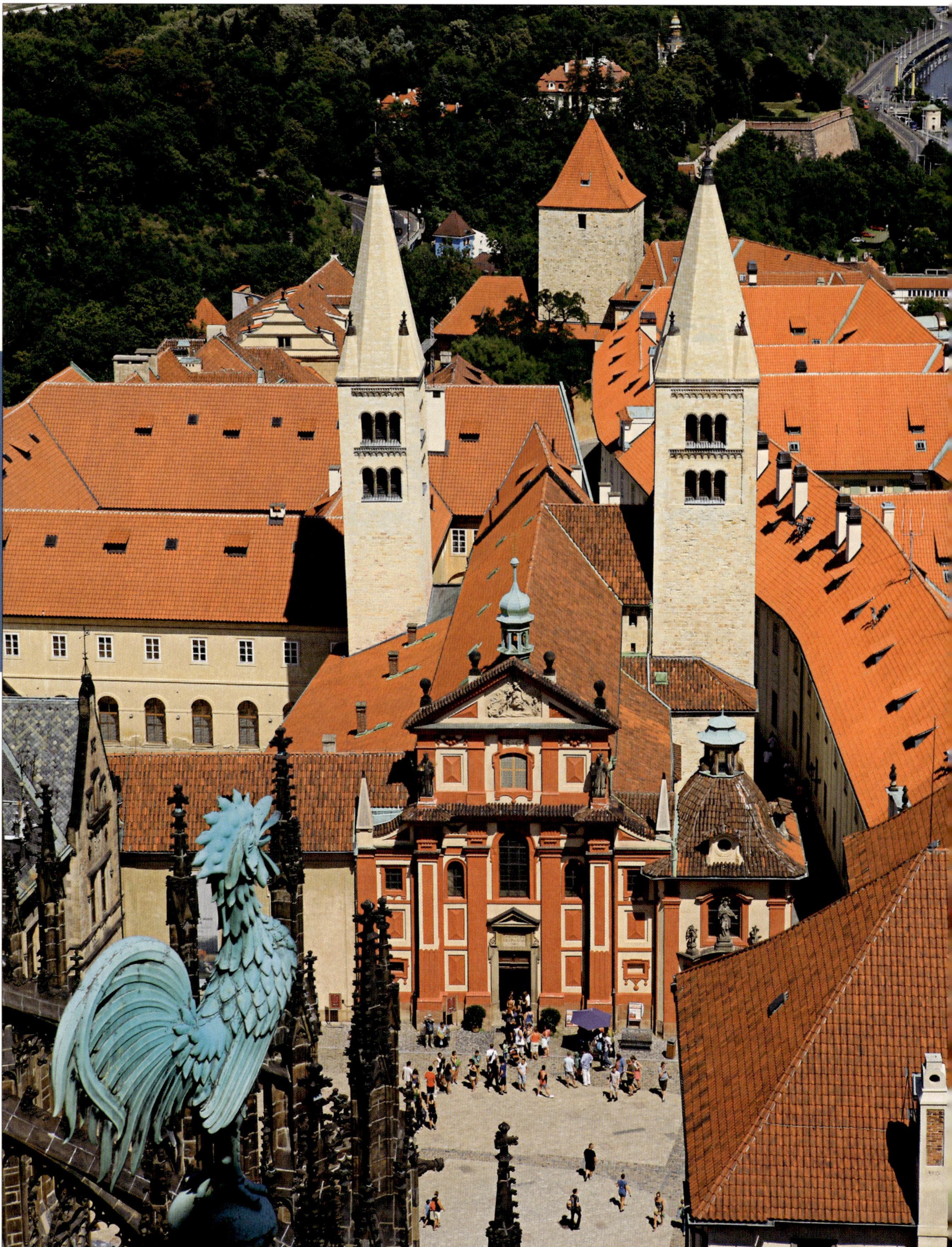

ST. GEORGE'S BASILICA

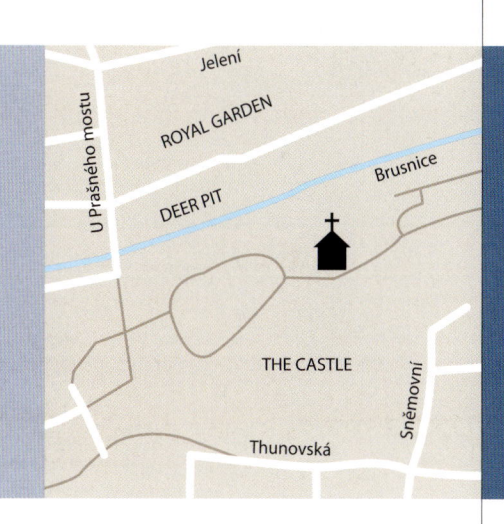

A pair of white towers completes the panorama of Prague Castle. They belong to the Romanesque three-aisle St. George's Basilica.

Castle, Prague 1 – Hradčany
Transport: Tram 1, 18, 22, 25 Prague Castle
Worship:
occasionally
920 founded
Around 1670 – completion of the Baroque facade
1888–1918 Purist reconstruction in the original Romanesque form

At the beginning of the tenth century, on the rocky promontory where Prague Castle stands today, there was only a small fortified settlement of the Přemyslid dynasty, accompanied by small churches. They were founded by Duke Vratislaus I and dedicated to St. George. However, by the year 920, in place of the original church, the three-aisle Basilica had already begun to grow, and after the year 973 it became a part of the Benedictine monastery for women, which Duke Boleslaus II had founded.

In 1142, the basilica was damaged during a siege of the castle by the army of Conrad of Znojmo. During the repairs, the temple was lengthened and a southern tower was added to the previously built northern tower. The South tower was complemented by the chapel of St. Ludmila and an apse at the end of the basilica. The North tower was later named Eva, while the South was named Adam. In the thirteenth century, the basilica was lengthened again, this time to the west; about a hundred years later, a new chapel of St. Ludmila was built which covered the apse by the aisle on the southern side, as well as the original chapel of St. Ludmila by the tower. The basilica, which is made of a typical light-colored marlstone ashlar, preserved its original Romanesque appearance until it was later disturbed by a Baroque façade. The façade was built around 1670; its crea-

General view from the Cathedral of St. Vitus. In the picture, the differing widths of each tower are clearly visible.

tor is thought to be Francesco Caratii. The facade features a centrally-placed relief depicting a battle between St. George and a dragon, while the side of the facade features statues of Duke Vratislaus with a beatified Mlada in his shield. Mlada was the sister of Boleslaus II and the founder of the women's Benedictine monastery. The statues come from the workshop of the sculptor Jan Jiří Bendl, while the handwriting on them is of the early Baroque style. It's worth noting that Mlada is holding a crown in her hand, whereas Vratislaus, as the founder of the temple, is holding its model.

The battle of St. George with the dragon is another artistic gem, actually a Renaissance portal added to the South temple wall, facing the narrow, downward-sloping Jiřská street. The relief of St. George in the tympanum portal was most likely created shortly after the year 1500 by the architectural ironworks of Benedict Ried, appointed by Vladislav Jagellon to repair the, at that time, substantially derelict Prague Castle and to finish the Cathedral of St. Vitus. The Renaissance portal was moved to a small garden, separated from Jiřská street by a stone wall and a small iron fence.

This minute detail endows the otherwise hulking construction with its own special magic. We shouldn't overlook the chapel of St. John of Nepomuk, added on to the right side of the façade. It was built in approximately 1720, following a design by František Maximilián Kaňka. The sculptural decorations originate from the workshop of Ferdinand Maximilián Brokoff. The interior of the basilica is, in comparison with Gothic, Renaissance and Baroque sanctuaries, frostily destitute and unfeeling. It bears typical features of Romanesque architecture, in which moderation and restraint dominate much more than opulence. The colossal stone walls, completely barren; the unadorned plain beam ceilings and narrow, small windows allowing an imperceptible amount of light into the gloom of the basilica; together, they create an oppressive atmosphere, forcing visitors into silent reflection and contemplation. The massive Gothic tomb with the remains of Duke Vratislaus, placed in these hushed spaces, reminds one of Noah's ancient ark. Besides his remains, there are also the remains of Boleslaus II and St. Ludmila. There is a curious legend associated with the placement of

The Square by St. George's

the remains of this female saint, murdered at Tetín castle, located on a rocky promontory looming over the Berounka river: her remains should have been deposited in the basilica, in accordance with the wishes of Duke Wenceslas. That should have happened in year 925. At that time, naturally, the basilica still hadn't been consecrated. Perhaps precisely because of this, the grave intended for Ludmila suddenly flooded with water as if the female saint didn't want to lie in the soil of an unconsecrated temple. The water only disappeared when the Regensburg bishop consecrated the basilica, and St. Ludmila was finally able to lie within its walls.

There is another, much more gruesome legend connected with St. George's Basilica. Some young sculptor fell unhappily in love with an impoverished girl, possibly named Bridget (but that's not important). The hot-tempered boy suffered from extreme jealousy, which propelled him to commit a blood-curdling deed. The sculptor murdered the poor girl, and was then captured and sentenced to death on the executioner's block. In the last days of his life, in the darkness of his dungeon cell, awaiting his execution, the young murderer then created – perhaps in a display of his penitence, or perhaps, conversely, in wrathful, diabolical rapture – a ghoulish, hair-raising creation: a statuette of a rotting, decomposing corpse with snakes squirming out of its guts. It can be seen today next to the altar, under the chancel in the arched crypt. Let us add that this ghastly tale has its roots in real events: at the dawn of the eighteenth century, a certain Italian sculptor named Bernardo Spinetti dwelled in Prague. Love blazed in his heart for a young maiden named Marie, the daughter of a castle gardener. Perhaps he became jealous, or maybe his love was unrequited; in any event, he was overcome with fury. One spring morning he stabbed her with a dagger, killing her. He was sentenced to death and also to have his hand cut off, the hand which had held the dagger. While waiting for his death, he carved the terrifying statuette, which is now called Bridget, but which he, however, called Futility. The Italian lover got lucky in the end though, and right on the executioner's block he unexpectedly received a pardon with the condition that for three years he would clean all the dung and filth from the streets of Prague.

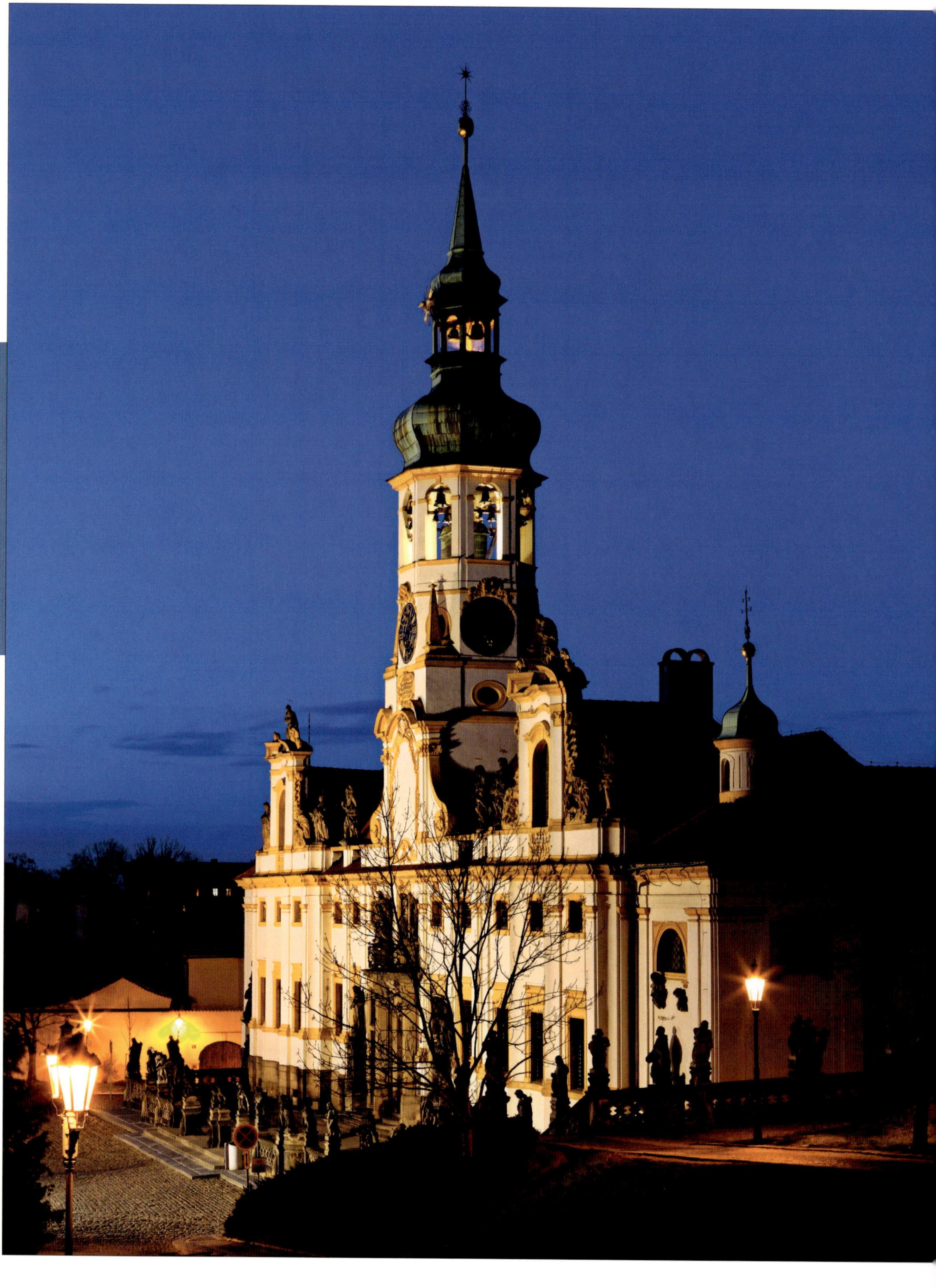

*It was May at that time,
a white moon stood above Loreta.
The clock tower rang one o'clock.*

J. Seifert

LORETTA

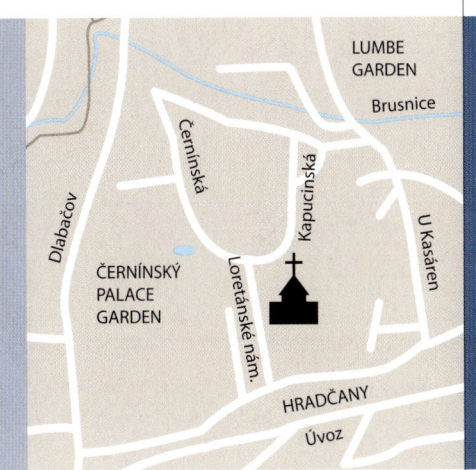

An important church complex from the late Baroque period, including the Church of the Nativity, a pilgrimage site, the Loretta treasure, and the Holy Hut of the Annunciation (Loreta).

Loretta Square 7, Prague 1 - Hradčany
Transport: Tram 22 Pohořelec
Worship:
Sat 7:30 am (in Santa Casa), Sun 6:00 pm (in the Church of the Nativity)
1626-1631 construction
18th century - completion of the Baroque facade

Not far from Pohořelec, under the gentle slope of Loreta Square, a huge Baroque complex named Loreta is situated. In the facade, there is a clock tower from which a picturesque stone staircase descends, guarded by the rigid face of an allegorical statue. Loreta is shaded by broad, branchy trees, behind which Černín Palace stretches out on top of a big hill. The small square is enclosed by the Capuchin monastery, around which a narrow street descends to the New World, a romantic clustering of streets under the Hradčany bulwark.

Construction on the Baroque Loreta complex was initiated in 1626, when the founding stone was laid of what is now known as the Holy Hut, which is situated in the middle of the compound and surrounded by multi-story cloisters. The Hut represents the symbolic center of an imaginary cross: the vertical line of the cross extends from the West, where the entrance for the complex is situated, to the East, where the Church of the Nativity is located. The horizontal line of the cross is formed by the chapels of St. František Serafin and Antonio Paduan.

With its growing significance as a pilgrimage site, Loreta was expanded and another chapel was built in the corner of the complex during the course of the seventeenth century. The original Nativity chapel was expanded into a spa-

Loreta chimes. The bells are stationary and are sounded with blows of hammers.

View of the façade building

▶ Spring mood at Loreta Square

▶▶ Aerial view of Loreta, in the axis of the façade the building Santa Casa and the Pilgrimage Church of the Nativity behind it are visible.

cious church. Kryštof Dienzenhofer significantly contributed to the architectural design of the entire compound; he was officially recognized for the Baroque reconstruction of the church and the West façade of Loreta, whose completion was taken over by his son Kilian Ignac after his death in 1722. Kilian also designed the terrace and balustrade in front of Loreta. The Church of the Nativity was finished in 1735 by Johann Georg Aichbauer.

In 1737, the Church of the Nativity was consecrated. However, work on its rococo-style interior continued through the following year. Noteworthy features include the replica of the Renaissance painting, *The Adoration of Jesus*, reminiscent of the painting school of F. Lippi, and the statues of St. Jachym, God's Father and angels or the side altars of St. Marcie and St. Felicissima with a reliquary showcase. Visitors here can also admire a vault mural, *Christ's Sacrifice in the Temple* by V.V. Reiner (1698-1743). We also shouldn't overlook the organ, which was created between 1734 and 1738 by F. Karter and K. Weltzer, and thereby replaced the original instrument made by L. Spiegel in the year 1718.

In the cloister, lining the vestibule of Loreta, we can also take in what is known as the "Loreta treasure", consisting of liturgical items from the sixteenth through eighteenth centuries. One of the most valuable artifacts is a diamond monstrance, called "the Prague Sun", completed at the end of the seventeenth century. It is encrusted with more than six thousand diamonds. An integral part of the Hradčany atmosphere is also the melody of the Loreta chimes, calling pilgrims to prayer each hour. A Lesser Town businessman named Eberhard from Glauchov had them built for Loreta by a bell-founding master from Amsterdam named Claude Fremy, who created this work between 1683-1691. In 1695, the bells were consecrated and the chimes were placed in the clock tower. The Roman Emperor and the Bohemian and Hungarian King, Leopold I, was the patron of the first bell. The ringing melody rang out from Loreta for the first time above Hradčany and Lesser Town roofs on August 15th, 1695.

The true spiritual center of Loreta, however, is formed by the Holy Hut (Santa Casa), a replica of the Nazareth home

25

of the Lord's Annuciation. The original torso of the Nazareth construction was dismantled by pilgrims at the end of the thirteenth century and its parts were transported to the Italian Loreta. The transfer of the Holy Hut, which was the subject of artistic interpretations in paintings and sculptures of angels carrying the Nazareth building, caused the establishment of the so-called Loreta cult, which constantly imitated the architectural design of the Italian model. Prague Loreta thereby joined the ranks of other Loretta pilgrimage sites in Italy, Austria and Germany, whose boom occurred from the second half of the sixteenth century. The first, mandatory, act was to surround the Holy Hut with Renaissance paneling with richly embossed ornamentation, which transformed it into a reliquary. The interior of the Holy Hut is divided into two spaces by a barred partition. Behind the partition we can see a statue of the Loreta Virgin Mary, placed in an elaborate, richly ornamented silver frame from the year 1671, as well as liturgical items, candlesticks and reliquary from the seventeenth century. The author of the fresco painting, encased in a rustic brick lining, is F. Kunz, who created it in 1795.

Pilgrims will be surprised by the scene in one dark corner of the Loreta cloister: on the cross there is a young woman, whose face is covered by a thick, black beard. This is Saint Starosta, defender of the unfairly condemned. Her unyielding father wanted to wed her to a merciless Muslim ruler. The young girl desperately prayed that God would rescue her from the marriage, and that a thick beard would grow on her face by morning. Her prayer was granted, but although the wedding did not occur, Starosta's father punished her by crucifixion. Starosta became one of the gloomy motifs of the Loretta cycle *Kammený most* poetry collection by Jaroslav Seifert, Prague poet and winner of the Nobel prize for literature (1901 – 1986):

Two woman's hands, translucent
I see them raised to the sky
On the cross a girl: tranquil peace
On a face from which a moustache creeps
In her hands, three spikes sunk deep
(…)
God gave her growth on the mouth
A beard falling to her belt did sprout
The executioner up with cross, her led
So that closer to Christ she'd be in death
And to His face, filled and glowing

27

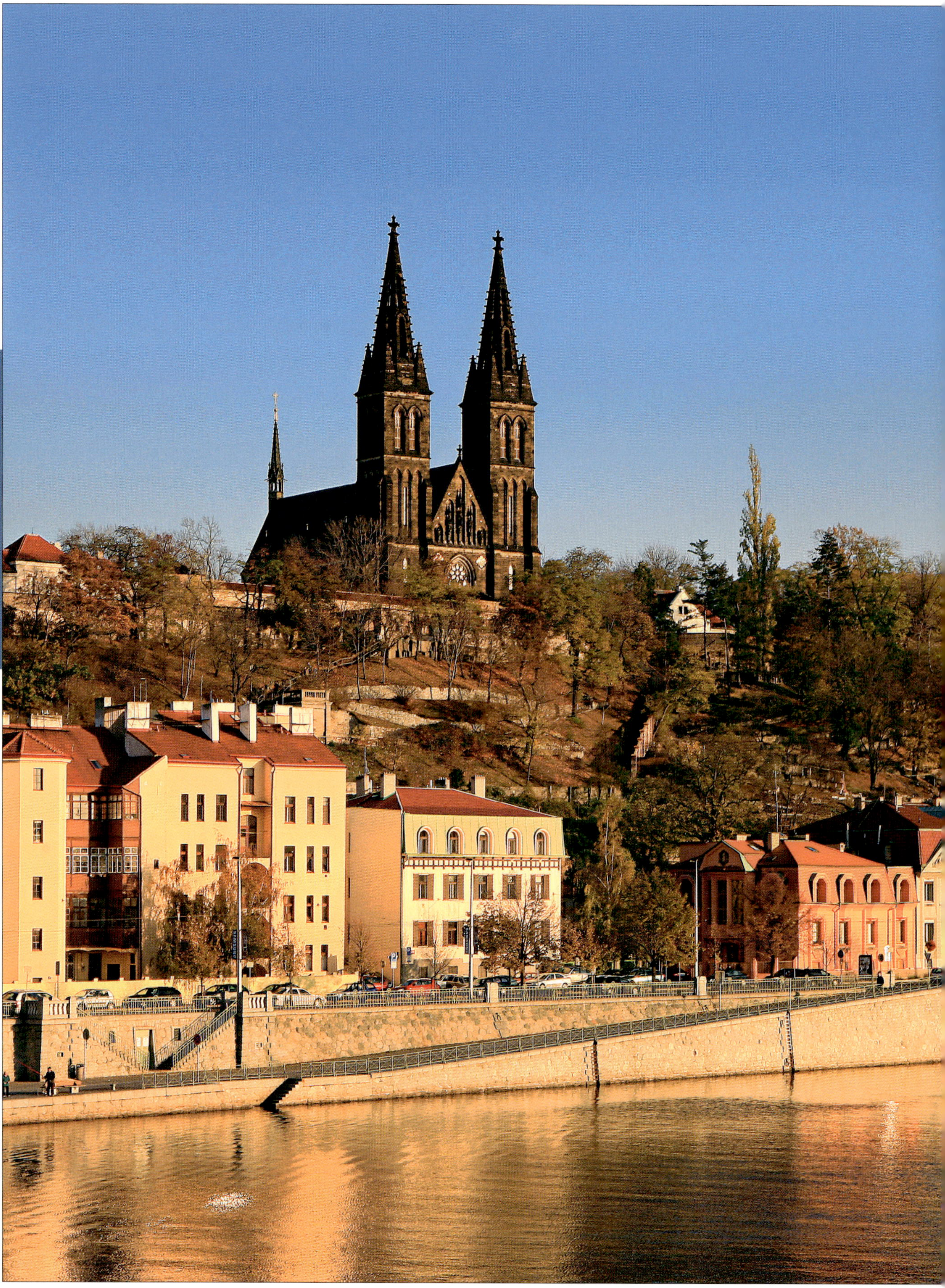

THE CHURCH OF ST. PAUL AND ST. PETER

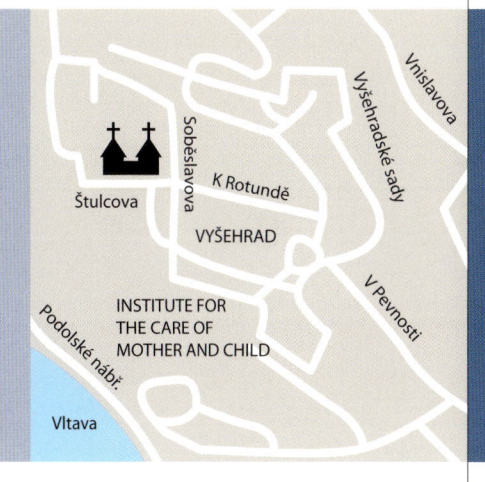

The massive, capitular neo-Gothic church on the cliffs of Vyšehrad is a spiritual and mythical site of Czech history and the formation of the Czech kingdom. After Prague Castle, it is the most significant historical site in Prague.

Štulcova st., Prague 2 - Vyšehrad
Transport: Metro C Vyšehrad
Worship:
Thu 6:00 pm, Sun 9:00 am
Built in 1369
1576 Renaissance reconstruction
1707-1729 Baroque reconstruction
1885-1903 Neo-Gothic reconstruction

The mythical and oldest spiritual center of Prague is not, after all, Prague Castle with St. Vitus Cathedral and St. George's Basilica, but rather Vyšehrad, lying atop the tall Vyšehrad cliffs above the Vltava, which right in that place - as the legend goes - is bottomless...The beginnings of the local castle fall into the class of myths and legends, like the information about the first sanctuaries which were built here. Today, Vyšehrad is dominated by the mammoth neo-Gothic Church of St. Peter and St. Paul, with the adjacent Slavín cemetery, where some distinguished Czech figures lay.

The roots of the temple of St. Peter and St. Paul go back, of course, to the reign of Duke Vratislaus II, who abandoned Prague Castle in approximately 1070 and relocated to Vyšehrad. With the coronation of Vladislaus II in the year 1140, Vyšehrad ceased to be the seat of sovereign power, which shifted back to Prague Castle. However, it remained the spiritual and primarily mythical epicenter of the city. That is also the reason why the temple of St. Peter and St. Paul was rebuilt in an early Gothic style, though at a very high cost, after the devastating fire of 1249. This reconstruction lasted almost fifty years, and another modification of the sanctuary, already over one hundred meters long, was initiated by Queen Eliška Přemyslovna in approximately 1330. Five original pillars have been preserved from this

View of the church of St Peter and Paul from the Vyšehrad orchards

The Church of Peter and Paul with Vyšehrad rock, from which, according to a legend, a knight on horseback named Horymír jumped to escape from prison. A number of Czech national legends are associated with Vyšehrad.

▶ The Neo-Gothic tympanum in the facade with a motif of the Last Judgment by S. Zálešák (1902)

time. Under the rule of Charles IV, when the light shoes and bag of Přemysl the Ploughman, the mythical founder of the royal Přemyslid dynasty, were supposedly stored as precious relics, the temple gained the form of a late Gothic three-aisle basilica with a continuous row of side chapels.

After top-quality Gothic modifications the proportions of the temple changed, and it became shorter in comparison with Romanesque design; however, its width was enlarged. The Romanesque parvis was demolished. At that time the temple was richly equipped. It was adorned with thirty altars and its cardinal spiritual and cultural significance was underlined by the fact that after his death on the 11th of December 1378, the body of Charles the IV was exhibited here.

In October of 1420, the Vyšehrad royal military company was being starved out by the Prague Hussites, and had decided to surrender if help from the Crusader's army of King Zigmund didn't arrive by the first of November at nine o'clock in the morning. Zigmund's army was severely delayed and the Vyšehrad company therefore surrendered to the Hussites. The Prague Hussites, who thereby took possession of Vyšehrad castle without a fight, entered into its fortifications and the excited mob destroyed and looted everything they could. The king's palace was burned to ashes, the Church of St. Peter and St. Paul was demolished, and the crypt of Přemysl was also filled in, along with the graves of the oldest Czech kings. Vyšehrad fell into utter ruin and decimation.

Only at the end of the fifteenth century did the Vyšehrad chapter in history resume; the wrecked temple was provisionally repaired and consecrated again, though in 1503 the badly repaired vault of the church collapsed. The temple was again overgrown with weeds for decades, and continued to fall into decay. It was only in 1565 that at least a partial repair of the sanctuary was undertaken by the Italian builder Ulrich Aostalis, who made the central aisle. In 1654, Vyšehrad was rebuilt into a military fort with a massive brick bulwark which surrounds it to this day. The ruins of the original buildings were demolished but the temple remained, and in 1678 also acquired a Baroque belfry. From years 1707–1711 the temple underwent expensive repairs on the basis of plans drawn up by Jan Blažej Santini-Aichl,

31

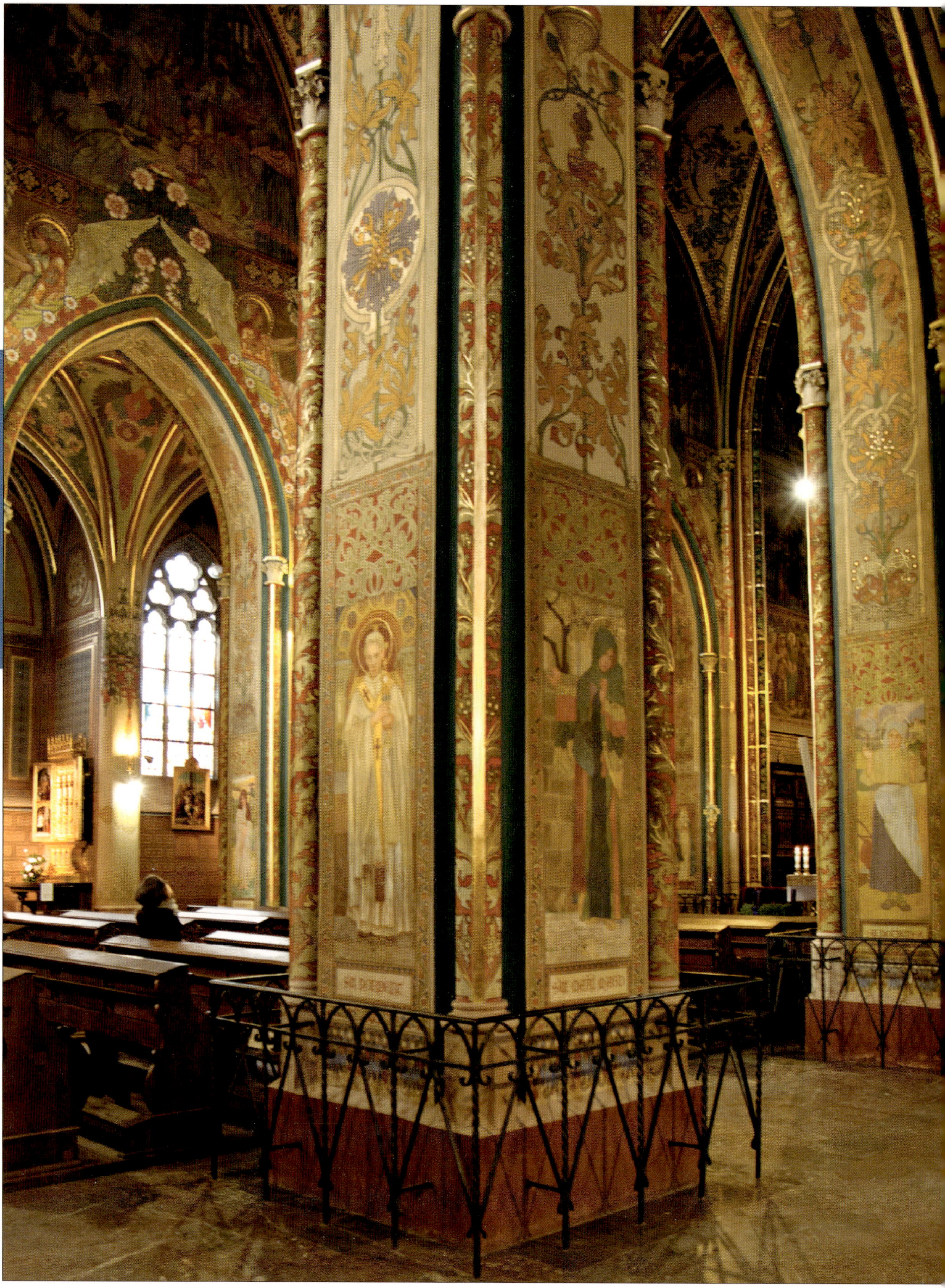

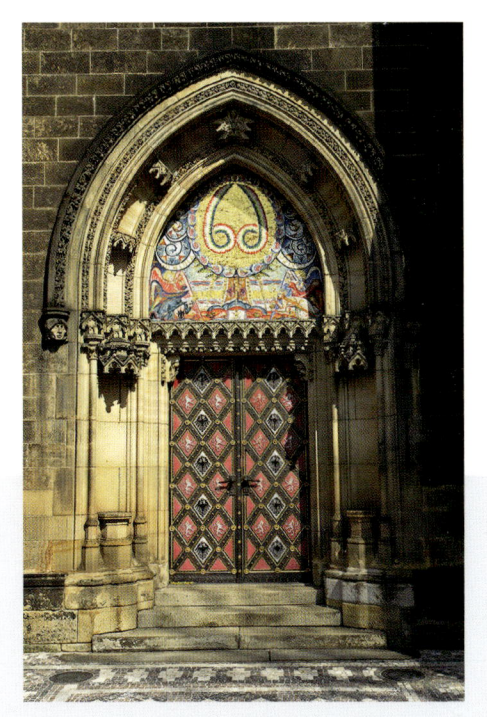

The entry portals feature a modern mosaic with motifs of the letters alpha and omega by L. Šindelář (not installed until 1993).

◀ View of the interior

The capitular Church of St. Peter and Paul, the west facade before re-gothization (B. Roubalík, before 1885)

and after additional repairs in years 1723–1729, it gained a Baroque visage. The original Gothic vault was replaced by a dome, though from the outer perspective of the covered saddle-shaped roof top, the temple was missing a tower, whose position was occupied by a belfry. However, as the significance of Vyšehrad as a military fort gradually subsided, it was realized that the architectural design of the whole site wasn't exactly harmonious, and that it was necessary to consider its reworking.

In the second half of the nineteenth century, the Vyšehrad cemetery, from which today's Slavin originated, was repaired first of all, so that the deanship and capitular home could also be rebuilt. An orchard was planted on Vyšehrad and the whole space lost its military character. The rebuilding of the temple in a neo-Gothic style, which began in 1880 and lasted another fourteen years, was undertaken by Josef Mocker. The Baroque belfry was likewise torn down. In 1898, during the celebration of the fiftieth anniversary of the rule of Emperor Franz Joseph I, the temple acquired a wall mural as well as neo-Gothic furniture. Then,

in 1903, Rocker's pupil František Mikš built two sixty-meter neo-Gothic towers alongside the facade. Today's incarnation of the Vyšehrad temple is connected with elements of the Gothic basilica from the time of Charles IV and Rocker's neo-Gothic reconstruction.

In the interior of the temple we primarily see neo-Gothic furniture, which replaced the original Baroque altars and other equipment. From those, actually, only the benches in the chancel from the end of the seventeenth century remained, as well as the Baroque altar paintings from the workshop of Karel Škréta Jr., which were taken down from the original altar and placed on the temple walls as hanging paintings. The neo-Gothic central altar originated in 1887. It is decorated by a relief of a woodcarver's rendering of the prophets St. Cyril, St. Methodius, St. Peter, and St. Paul. The top passage of the altar ends in the Calvary. On the south side of the choir we shouldn't overlook the original painting of *The Assumption of the Virgin Mary;* then, in the presbytery, there is a relief of John of Nepomuk. In the north aisle is the first of five chapels, devoted to the Seven Sorrows of

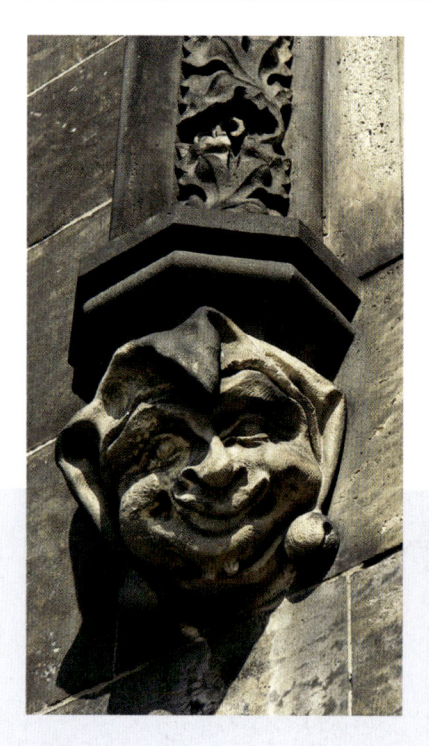

Decorative neo-Gothic chapiter under the supporting ribs of the presbytery arch

▶ The panorama of Vyšehrad forms a natural counterbalance to Prague Castle, which is located on the opposite river bank.

the Virgin Mary. Another chapel, dedicated to St. John the Baptist, is accompanied by a painting of this Saint. A depiction of St. Martin, which has a hanging painting, adorns the altar in the next chapel, the the Chapel of St. Ann, created by Škréta Jr. The last chapel in the north aisle is dedicated to St. František. The wall enclosing the north aisle is decorated with restored Baroque wall murals representing the Vyšehrad legend of the devil's pillar. Three massive stone fragments have been preserved from this. They are currently located in the Karlach orchard behind the Vyšehrad cemetery, and even now it isn't clear how or why this pillar even got to Vyšehrad in the first place.

A legend offers one explanation: A long time ago, after the completion of the temple, a mischievous servant of God was discovered within the group of priests. He was more interested in gambling with cards than in worship and service. However, because he had mostly bad hands, he usually lost at cards. When he didn't have enough to cover what he had lost and was almost broke, he sold his soul to the Devil in order to have better luck with his card playing. In time, however, he realized what exactly he had done, and what was awaiting him after death. He even prayed to God for advice. God's servant, St. Peter, advised him to demand one of the pillars from St. Peter's temple in Rome from the Devil. If the Devil didn't bring the pillar before morning Mass, his power would be broken. The priest declared his wish and the Devil flew off to Rome. However, he didn't head for St. Peter's temple as requested, but for another Roman church, S. Maria Trastevere. There he broke off one of the pillars and set back for Vyšehrad. Somewhere above Venice, St. Peter flew out from behind the clouds toward the Devil, and took the pillar from him and threw it in a Venice lagoon. The Devil dove down into the water, and firmly clutched the pillar with his claws. However, Peter again intervened and again threw the pillar in the water. Although the Devil yet again fished it out of the water, he knew he could no longer make up the lost time. The priest finished the Mass, and the exasperated demon flung the pillar down at the roof of the church and it broke into three pieces. And we'd like to add that in the Roman church of S. Maria Trastevere, one supporting pillar is in fact missing…

Historians and archaeologists are somewhat more prosaic in their explanation of the pillar's origin. It could be the remnants of an ancient time-telling pillar or an element of the original Vratislaus church. Also interesting is the theory that the pillar came from a Hussite battering ram which broke, and the pieces of which were then launched from a catapult by the Hussites to attack the walls of Vyšehrad. (One other intriguing detail is that one of the Hussite commanders was actually named Devil!)

Let us now take a look at the South aisle, and at the same time the accompanying fifth chapel. The first chapel is dedicated to St. Climent, whose portrayal on a hanging painting originates from the workshop of Karel Škréta, Jr. We should also be careful not to overlook the so-called coffin of St. Longinus, a stone sarcophogus from the turn of the twelfth century. Legend has it that the remains of St. Longinus were brought from Rome to Prague in this massive stone chest, by which Vyšehrad is connected with the mythology of the Holy Grail. Today, however, historians rule out any sort of link with St. Longinus and are inclined to be of the opinion that in reality it's a sarcophagus of one of the Přemyslids.

Another south aisle chapel is dedicated to the Czech patron and is adorned by a painting of St. Wenceslas by Škréta, similar to the next chapel, the chapel of St. Mary Magdalene, which is complemented by a portrayal of John the Evangelist. In the Chapel of the Virgin Mary of the Rain, there is a very valuable copy of a board painting from the third quarter of the fourteenth century. The painting allegedly belongs to Charles IV and its acknowledged owner is also Emperor Rudolph II. The painting was carried during religious proceedings on hot, dry days and almost always brought the much-needed rain. The last chapel of the south aisle is dedicated to Saint Joseph, the frescoe mural fragments dating back to the Gothic period. At the conclusion of the tour, if we leave the side aisle and return to the central aisle we can't miss the large wall mural decorating the upper part of the aisle. It was created in 1898, commissioned to the Austrian painter Karl Jobst. Featuring scenes from the life of Christ and the patron saints, the mural was produced for the fiftieth anniversary of the rule of Emperor Franz Joseph II.

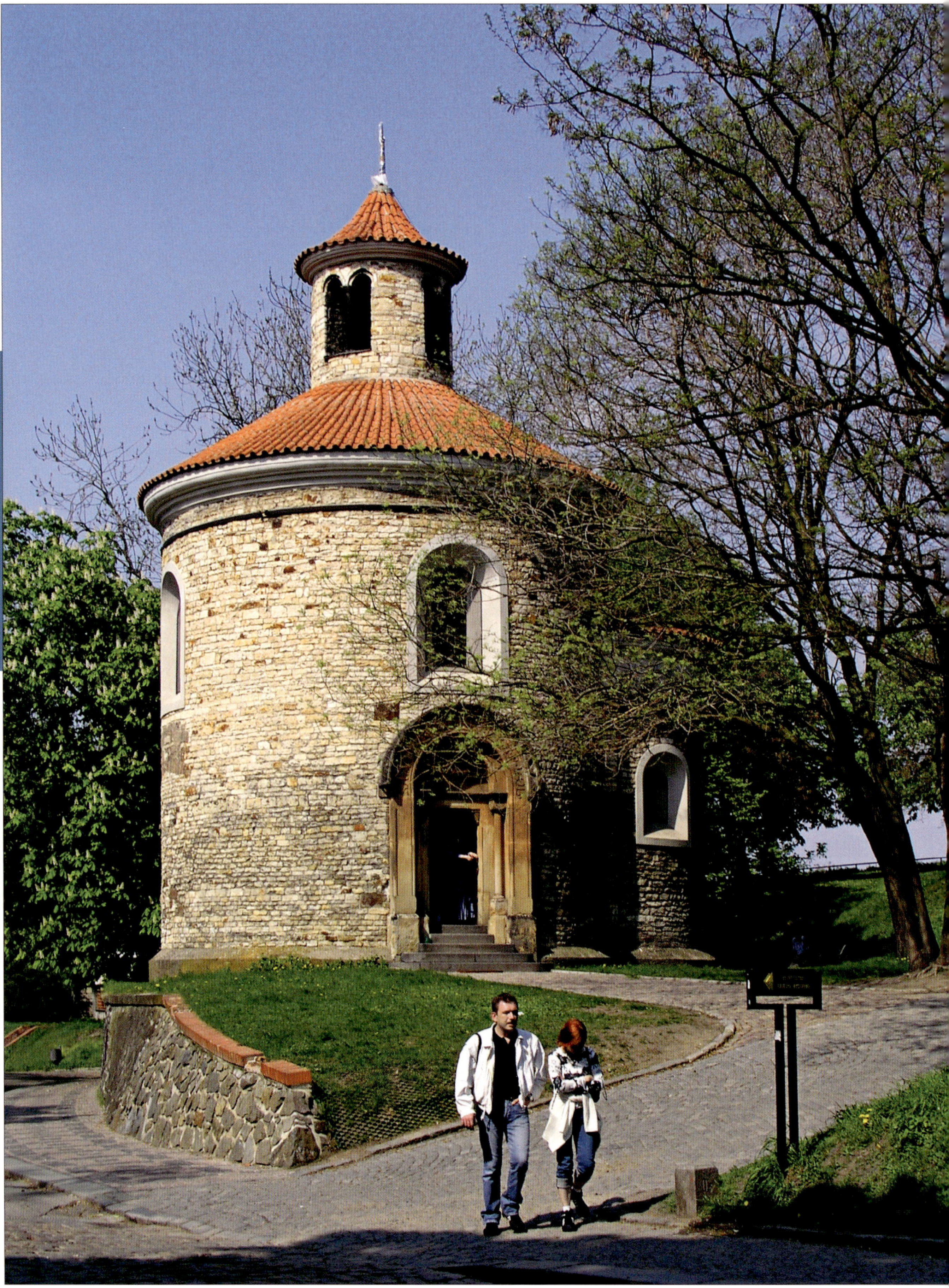

ST. MARTIN'S ROTUNDA

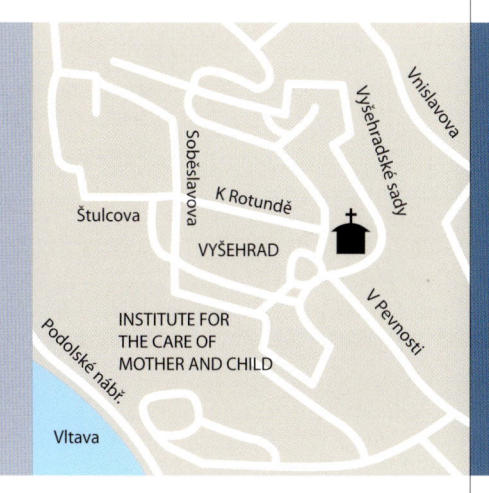

The oldest preserved historical site of a church in the area of Prague, a Romanesque rotunda on the romantic and historically meaningful Vyšehrad cliffs.

In the Fortress, Prague 2 – Vyšehrad
Transport: Metro C Vyšehrad
Worship:
Mon, Wed, Fri 6:00pm, Sun 9:00 am
Built in the 11th century
1878–80 renewal, portal extension

If we go through the massive Leopold Gate to Vyšehrad, our attention is captured by a small hill-top Romanesque rotunda. In front of us is the oldest surviving church in Prague, dedicated to St. Martin. The rotunda was built in approximately 1070, when the Czech territory was ruled by King Vratislaus II, and it was evidently a parish church.

After the Hussite War, the rotunda, as well as many other churches and monasteries, was ransacked; however, while the Hussite army made an impressive effort to destroy all of Vyšehrad's religious buildings after its victory over Zigmund the Emperor Crusader in 1420 in the battle at Vyšehrad, the temple of St. Peter and St. Paul and St. Martin's Rotunda – in spite of significant damage – survived in the end, although just barely. The rotunda also survived the Thirty Years' War, when Emperor Ferdinand III began to build a massive and complex fortification system. The rotunda thereby found itself directly in the center of the future fortification compound and was awarded the dubious role of powder house and storage house. After the Thirty Years' War it was consecrated a second time, but Joseph's reforms once again removed its spiritual function. The sword of Damocles hanging above St. Martin's rotunda swung alarmingly again in 1841, when it stood in the path of a newly planned road, connecting New Town

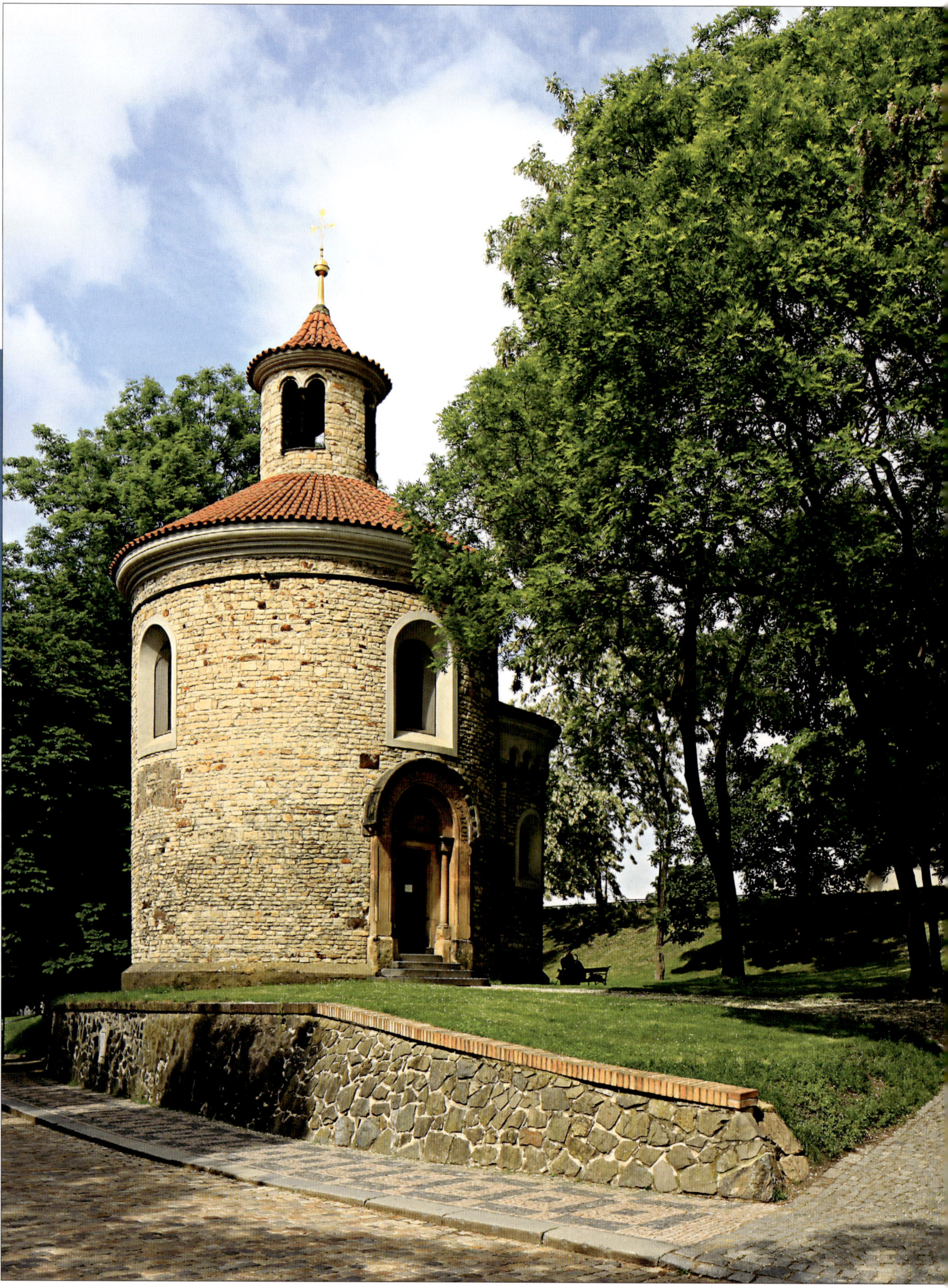

The Rotunda of St. Martin in a line drawing by B. Havránek

◄ The Rotunda of St. Martin, view from V Pevnosti street.

and the Pankrác quarter via a steep, ascending route. Only thanks to the intervention of Count Karel Chotka, the highest Czech burgrave, the road was slightly re-routed and the rotunda weathered out the road's construction without injury. In that period, however, it functioned as a residence for the poor; a new entrance was smashed open, and in the roof a hole for a chimney was punched out. Even the apse functioned as a kitchen.

In 1845, a Vyšehrad chapter purchased the rotunda, which they renovated in accordance with a design by Antonín Baum at the end of 1870. The exterior of the massive rotunda, with a diameter of six-and-a-half meters and with walls one meter thick, was spiced up by a neo-Romanesque portal with a motif inspired by the Vyšehrad codex, whose artistic interpretation can also be seen in the interior. A neo-Romanesque altar was decorated in Slivenec marble by the academic painter František Sequens.

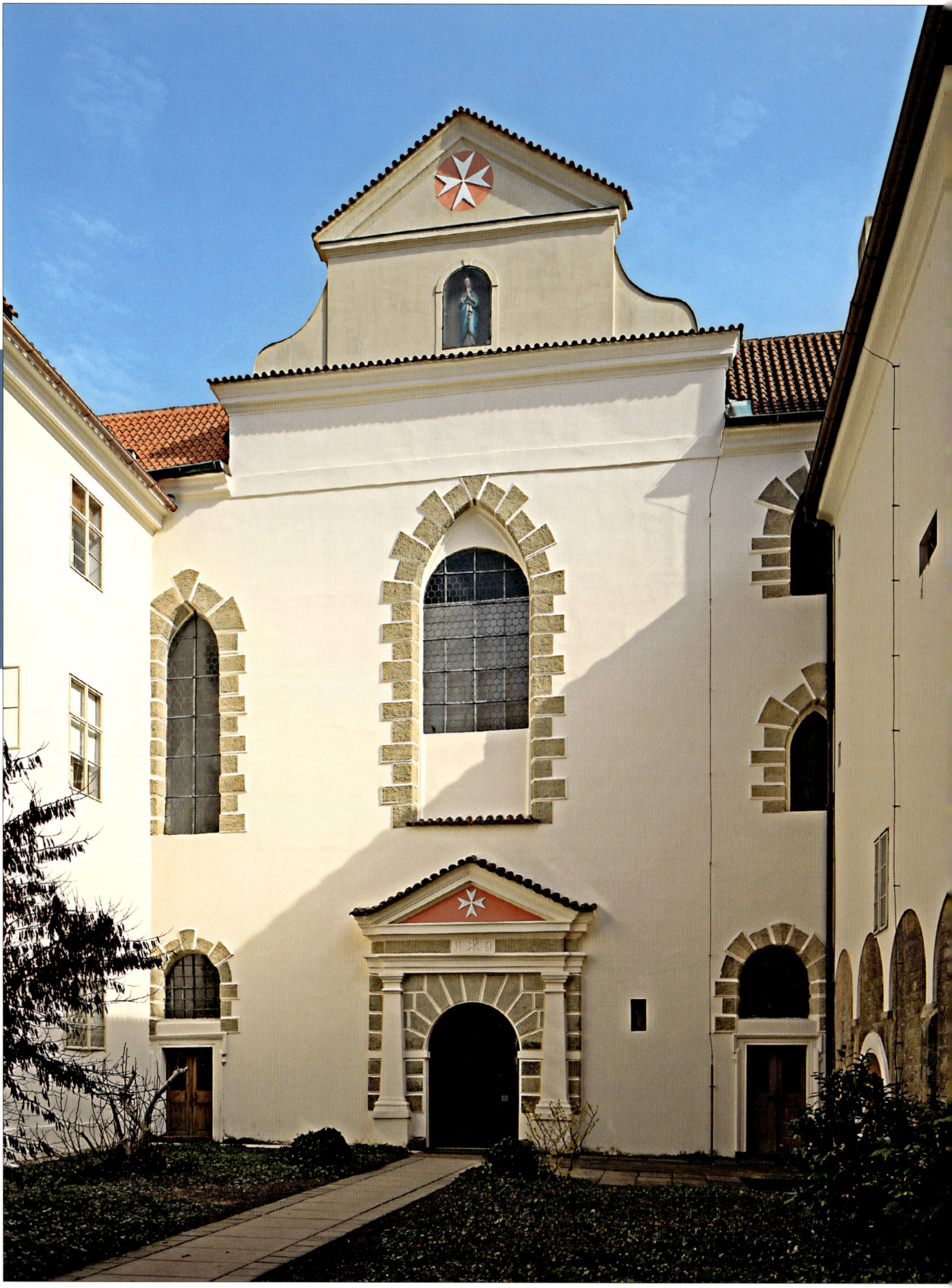

CHURCH OF THE VIRGIN MARY UNDER THE CHAIN, LESSER TOWN

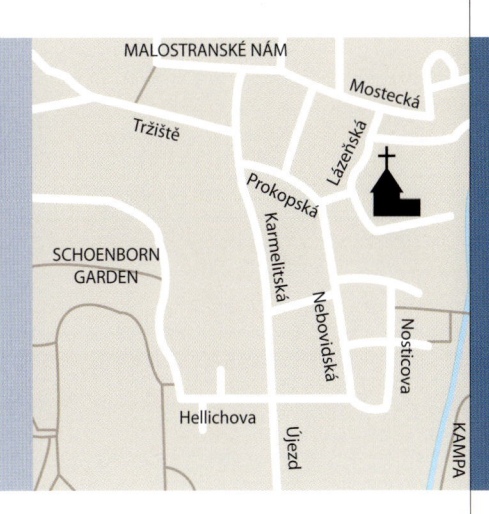

A Gothic church with Renaissance and Baroque reconstruction, belonging to the property of the Order of the Knights of Malta

Lázeňská st., Prague 1 - Malá Strana
Transport: Tram 12, 20, 22 Hellichova, Lesser Town Square
Worship:
Wed 5:30 pm, Sun 10:00 am
13th century - extension of the Gothic chancel to the original Basilica
16th /17th century construction

Losing one's way on a walk through the historical center of Prague and finding oneself in Velkopřevorské Square has two immediately pleasant side-effects. First, in the square itself visitors are reminded of the famous era of the Beatles and hippies by what is known as "Lennon's Wall", which is a symbolic grave of the famous musician. On the eighth of December every year, this wall becomes a place for holding vigil and remembering Lennon's tragic death; before 1989, it also provided an opportunity for Czechs to express their defiance and opposition to Communist rule. Secondly, provided the traveler goes across the square to its western corner and turns onto the short, narrow, winding Lázeňská Street, they will emerge in front of the stern, early Gothic Church of the Virgin Mary Under the Chain.

As far back as 1158-1170, King Vratislaus had a Johannite commenda built in this location - at that time still in the foreground of Judita's stone bridge, which spanned over the Vltava joining Lesser Town with Old Town, before the building of Charles' Bridge - to which a three-aisle Romanesque basilica was added a few years later, dedicated to the Virgin Mary. Back in those days, more precisely from the middle of the twelfth century, the basilica belonged to the Johannites, later the Order of the Knights of Malta, in whose hands the church remains today. The plan from the first half

Close up of the gate

View of the main nave and the altar

▶ A pair of Gothic towers, in the background a panorama of the Smetana and Masaryk embankment and the National Theatre

of the fourteenth century to rebuild the basilica into a larger Gothic temple was only partially successful. Only two towers in the Western façade and the presbytery were built in Gothic fashion. The Church of the Virgin Mary under the Chain was also nicknamed The End of the Bridge, on account of its location at the end of Judita's bridge; it was also called Malta, in light of its ownership by the Knights of Malta. Regardless of its name, the church was raided during the Hussite war in 1420 and burned down. It was also damaged by fire in 1503. So richly ornamented entry portal and the two 32-meter tall, prismatic tower built from massive marlstone ashlars are all that remains of its Gothic form. The church was already consecrated in the name of the Virgin Mary in the twelfth century, and in the end "Under the Chain" was added, reminiscent of the custom of closing the temple gate with a chain, which legend says was made of gold. The church's aisle was never finished and in the end was substituted by the presbytery, which over the years first acquired a Renaissance form and in around 1648, a Baroque form, thanks to the architect Carl Luragho.

As for notewothy artifacts in the interior of the church, there is an altar, which was made by the carver Jan Petr Wenda, dating back to 1740. The pulpit and two statues representing St. Raymond and St. Ubald also probably came from Wenda's workshop. In the north side wall of the aisle, we can also admire the remains of a medieval frescoe with scenes from the torture of St. Catherine.

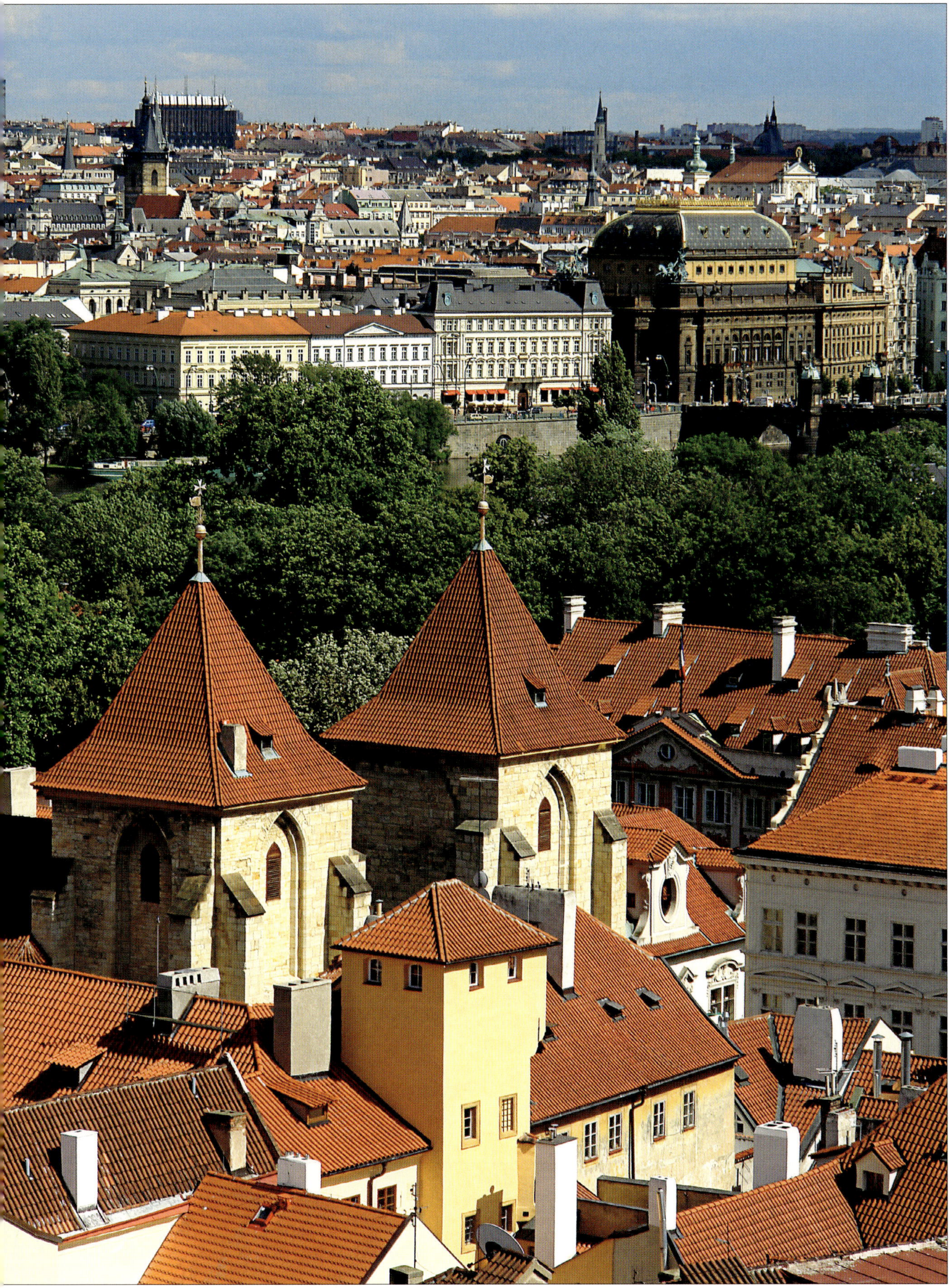

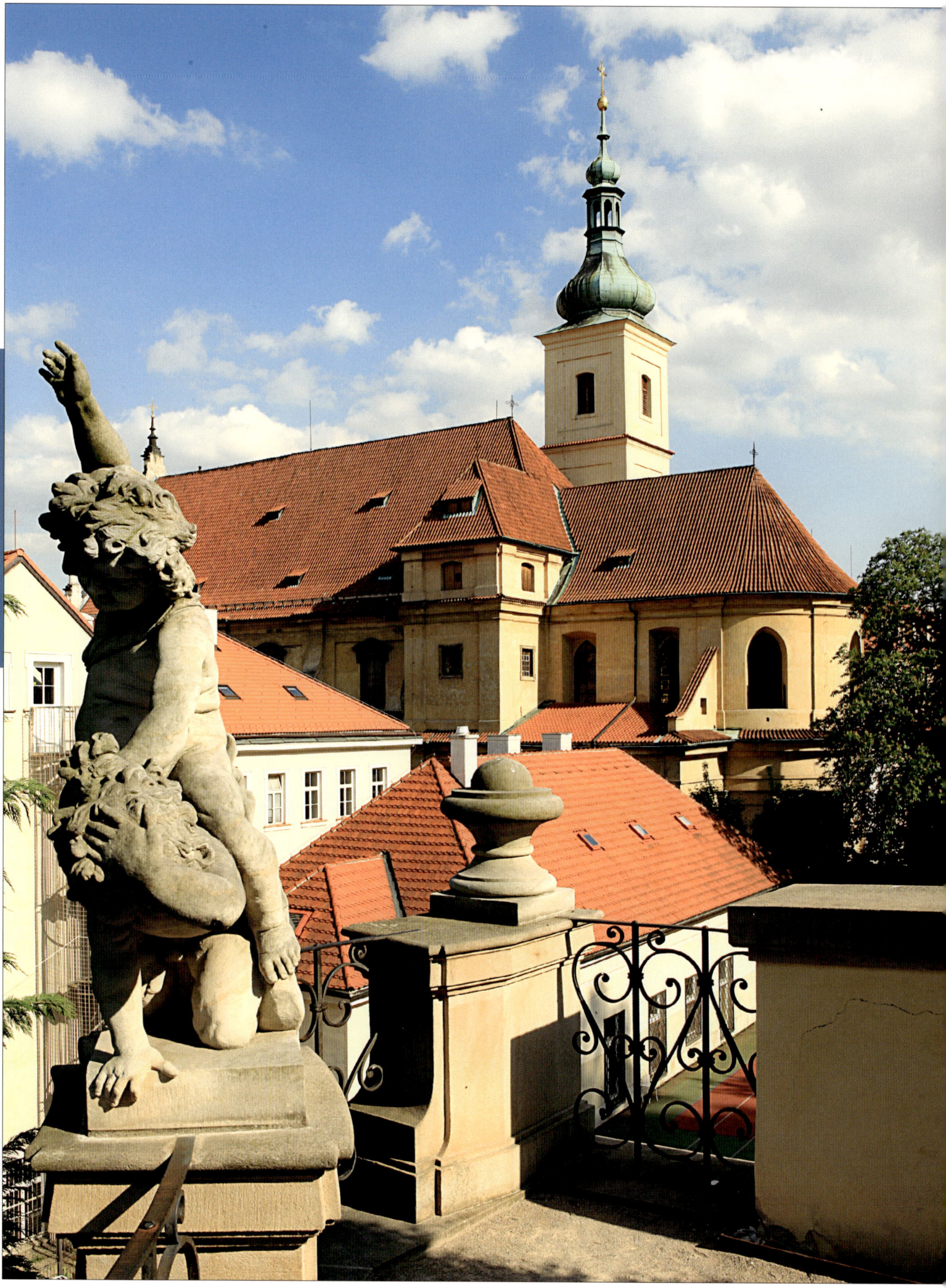

THE CHURCH OF OUR LADY OF VICTORY

One of the most well-known churches in Prague, with a statuette of the Infant Jesus of Prague

Karmelitská 9, Prague 1 - Malá Strana
Transport: Tram 12, 20, 22 Hellichova
Worship:
Mon-Wed 9:00 am 6:00 pm, Thu 9:00 am, 5:00pm, 6:00 pm, Fri 9:00 am, 6:00 pm, 7:30 pm, Sat 9:00 am, 5:00 pm, 6:00 pm, Sun 10:00 am, 12:00 pm, 5:00 pm, 6:00 pm, 7:00 pm (in various languages)
Built between 1611-1613
1624 dedicated to Our Lady of Victory
17th century - repeatedly rebuilt, tower completed

Part Renaissance and part early Baroque, the Roman-style Church of Our Lady of Victory and St. Anthony of Padua on Karmelitská Street in Lesser Town is certainly known by most Prague dwellers, as well as visitors, by the name "Infant Jesus of Prague". Today, there is a church with an adjacent monastery of barefoot Carmelites, poetically wedged under the slopes of Petřín; in the sixteenth century, however, it was the location of both the Jan Hus church, as well as a burial site for plague victims. At the beginning of the seventeenth century, the church was acquired by German Lutherans, who rebuilt it and dedicated it to the Holy Trinity, in reference to the Roman church S. Trinita dei Monti.

After the White Mountain Battle in 1620 and subsequent victory for the Catholic army, this Lutheran church was confiscated and handed over to the Barefoot (Discalced) Carmelites for their use. They, according to the wishes of Emperor Ferdinand II, consecrated the church as Our Lady of Victory. The patronage of the Virgin Mary was not chosen randomly, but as a reminder of the painting of Our Lady of Victory from Štěnovice. According to legend, on one October day in 1620, a Barefoot Carmelite, Dominic a Jesu Maria, found a mutilated painting, *Adoration of the Infant Jesus,* in a half-destroyed chapel not far from the village of Štěnovice near Plzeň, during the campaign of Duke Max-

46

Church of Our Lady Victorious with Prague Castle in the background

◄ Aerial view of the Church of Our Lady Victorious with Karmelitská Street

View of the main façade from Karmelitská street

imillian against the Czech Protestants. The Carmelite took the picture with him to the White Mountain Battle and used it to spur on his Catholic soldiers. The painting, which was later venerated as a manifestation of Our Lady of Victory, eventually wound up in Rome, where it was destroyed in a fire in the Church of St. Paul in 1833. Nevertheless, its Baroque copy found its home in our Lesser Town church, where we can view it in the top arc of the central altar.

In the first years of the post-White Mountain re-Catholicization, an extensive reconstruction of the church took place in which it gained its current Baroque appearance. The central aisle was changed so that it faces the west, and a new presbytery was built as well. In 1628, the Carmelites acquired a wax Renaissance statue of the infant Jesus, which should have brought peace and prosperity to the church as well as the monastery. In a certain sense that happened just in time, because Emperor Ferdinand shortly thereafter ordered the payment of a regular pension to the monastery along with the supplying of necessary food from the royal granary.

The statue of the Infant Jesus of Prague is actually an almost-50-centimeter-tall figurine, carved out of wood and with a wax surface. It is a portrayal of Jesus in his infancy. While his right hand is lifted in blessing, his left grips a globe topped by a cross. The statuette originated in Spain, and has since acquired a whole range of clothing which are used in accordance with the symbolic significance of the individual periods of the Christian year. It was made in the middle of the sixteenth century, and legend says that its maker was a monk to whom Jesus appeared in that form. It's also possible to believe another legend, which says that the statuette was first owned by St. Theresa from Jesus, the founder of the Barefoot Carmelites, who for that matter lived close to the Church of Our Lady of Victory – at Hradčanské Square.

The fact is, the statuette was received as a wedding gift from her mother by a Renaissance noblewoman named Polyxena Lobkowicz, who later donated it to the Carmelites. The statuette was almost immediately credited with having miraculous powers, and the Our Lady of Victory

Statue of the Infant Jesus

▶ View of the main nave

Church soon became a place of pilgrimage. The renown of the statuette saved it from the looting of Swedish soldiers. When the Swedes occupied Lesser Town in 1648 and shelled Old Town across the Vltava, the Swedish general issued an order of safe passage for the Carmelites, securing the church and monastery, where a military hospital was established in the meantime.

Apart from the statuette of the Prague Infant Jesus, it's also worth taking a look at the monumental Baroque painting, *Emperor Ferdinand II with Dominic a Jesu Maria praying to the Virgin Mary for victory in the battle of White Mountain*, created by the master Antonín Stevens from Steinfels in the year 1641. Another notable work is the painting by Matěj Zimprecht and the quartet of paintings by Peter Brandl, which adorn the side altar. It is also worth checking out the underground crypts, complete with mummified monks, as well as the tiny building behind the church, today a parish clerk's home, which served as a hermitage from the year 1659.

49

ALFONS MUCHA
exhibition
SALVADOR DALI
exhibition
RESTAURANT CAFE U TYNA

THE CHURCH OF OUR LADY BEFORE TÝN

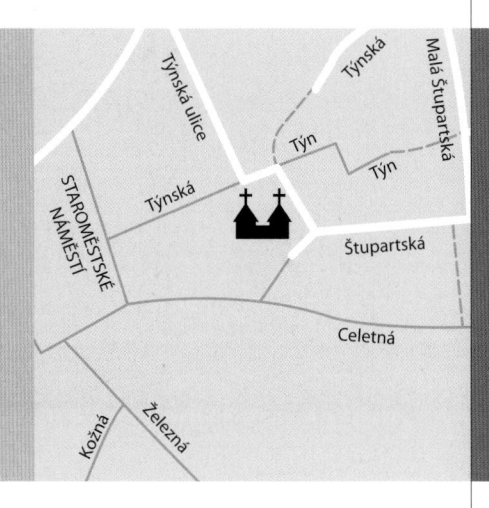

A noticeably dominant feature of Old Town Square, a massive three-aisle basilica with rich Baroque interior ornamentation.

Old Town Square, Prague 1 - Old Town

Transport: Metro A Staroměstská, Tram 17, 18 Staroměstská

Worship:
Mon-Fri 12:15 pm, Sat 8:00 am, Sun 9:30 am and 9:00 pm

1380 consecrated
1415 Utraquist
1620 Catholic again
1679 Baroque style interior

Old Town Square has been a witness to many key moments in the history of the Czech Republic. The bodies of those infected by the Plague were buried in the underground passageways under the square. There used to be a whipping post here, as well as the community gallows. Right here, at the beginning of the fifteenth century, the first Hussite storm commenced; it was also here, in 1620, that twenty-seven Bohemian lords were executed after the Czech Protestants lost the Battle of White Mountain. Here also an enraged mob knocked a Baroque Marian column to the ground as a gesture of separation from the Hapsburg monarchy in 1918; and on a cold and damp February morning in 1948, it was in this square that Klement Gottwald conveyed the message of the Communist takeover of Czechoslovakia. On all of these plus many other historical events, the massive, robust Gothic temple of Our Lady Before Týn stared down.

Along with Old Town Hall and the Orthodox Church of St. Nicholas, The Church of Our Lady Before Týn forms the unrivalled dominant feature of Old Town Square. The Týn church is situated to its eastern side and its base is, from the view of the square, hidden behind the façade of a city building, which covers the entrance to the church. In the first half of the twelfth century, a Romanesque rotunda dedicated to the Virgin Mary had already been built in its place, which

52

was probably commissioned to be built by Duke Spytihněv. On the church's eastern side, there is what is known as the Týn courtyard - "Ungelt", in which foreign buyers paid customs taxes for imported goods, and at the same time could also spend the night there in safety. The Týn courtyard was allegedly connected to the rotunda via a secret underground passageway, used by Duchess Ludmila. In the middle of the thirteenth century, a Romanesque three-aisle sanctuary and early Gothic church came into being there, whose foundation was discovered in the year 1886, under the cobblestones of St. Ludmila's chapel.

Then in the middle of the fourteenth century, on the site of the existing small church, a monumental temple began to be built there at the behest of Charles IV. Only a miniscule quantity of the initial construction documentation has survived, and the name of the first builder remains unknown. Nevertheless, Matyáš from Arras and Petr Parléř are listed as the primary builders of the top Gothic form of the temple, which from its inception became the parish church of Old Town. In spite of the fact that the church had already been consecrated back in the 1380s, work on its completion progressed very slowly. Around the year 1400, Petr Schmelzer and Otto Scheufler took charge of construction and, shortly before the Hussite rebellion, all three aisles were finished. However, the roof of the third aisle still hadn't been built (nor probably formed) and work on the western gable of the church and both towers hadn't been finished either.

After the Hussite storm - in 1415 - the church was taken over by the Ultraquists and Jacob from Stříbro founded his preaching site here. In the year 1419, at the request of King Wenceslas IV, the church was transferred into the hands of the Catholics; this, however, was just for a short time, because during the same year it was taken over by the Calixtines. From the year 1427, John Rokycana preached and occupied the role of priest here. His cup tilted towards the nobility, and he was chosen as archbishop in 1435 by the townspeople and the clergy, however without living to see his confirmation of his office by the Church. After the defeat of the Hussites in the summer of 1436, he was welcomed by Emperor Zigmund into the church, though the gratitude didn't last and less than a year later he lost the Týn parish house.

After the conclusion of the religious wars, it was finally time to complete the central aisle, which was still waiting for its roof frame. In the year 1437, wood was placed in Old Town Square for this purpose; however, Emperor Zigmund decided to use it for another purpose. The wood was used

M.R.A.
MAGNÆ URBIS HUIUS TUTELARI
SUPER CŒLOS OMNES ASSUMPTÆ
HÆC ARA POSITA EST DICATA
ANNO A VIRGINEO EJUS PARTU
M.D.C. XLIX.

A view of Týn Church from Týn Court (Ungelt)

◄◄ View of Old Town Square with Týn Church

◄ The main altar with an image of the Assumption of the Virgin Mary by Karel Škréta

instead to build a large gallows, upon which John Roháč perished along with 50 of his followers, who Zigmund arrested after the capture of Sion castle, the last site of the Hussite resistance. The church waited for its roof for another twenty years. Once again, a large stack of wood appeared in Old Town Square, which was intended for use during the wedding of the young king Ladislav the Posthumous. The king, however, died unexpectedly – the wedding didn't take place, and the suddenly available wood was immediately utilised for building the church roof.

Under the reign of the Ultraquist George of Poděbrady, whose heart was finally buried here, building continued: a roof was put on the central aisle, and in the year 1463 its gable was built, with a statue of George of Podebrad with an open, gilded chalice as a Hussite symbol. The chalice, however, also served as the ideal place for a nesting stork! The resulting mess, including snakes, lizards and rats which the stork carried to its babies in the nest (and which fell from the nest to "decorate" the front of the church), eventually led to the decision to seal up the chalice. At that time, the north tower was rising towards the sky, while the south wasn't finished until the reign of Vladislaus Jagellon in approximately 1511. The massive, prismatical towers were built from black ashlars with distinctively pointed, octagonal roofs and hemmed in with terraces with small spires in the corners. They now soar above Old Town Square to a height of eighty meters. In the end, the church was completed in the form of a three-aisle Gothic basilica with a massive, gabled central aisle, enclosed on the eastern side by a presbytery.

After the defeat of the Czech Protestants at the Battle of White Mountain in the year 1620, and after the execution of the 27 Bohemian lords, whose heads were hung on the terraces of the Old Town Bridge Towers, the Týn church fell once again into the hands of the Catholics. It's therefore no wonder that the statue of the Ultraquist King George of Poděbrady was removed from the gable above the central aisle in 1623, as well as the chalice. The whole affair had a somewhat peculiar, diverse character: under the leadership of John Ctibor Kotva, the canon of St. Vitus, several students from the Jesuit seminar set off to Týn under the cloak of night. They climbed up to the church gables, taking the chalice and the statue of King George, and – perhaps accidentally or maybe intentionally – they threw them down onto the ground. About three years later, an almost three-meter tall statue of the Madonna was placed into the available place where the chalice had been. The niche left from the statue of King George remained empty. Other symbols of the Ultraquists were also removed from the church, and the grave of John Rokycana was also destroyed. His bones, along with the preserved heart of George of Poděbrady, were burned in the square.

The Thirty Years' War signaled a new chapter for the Týn church. In the autumn of 1631, religious emigrants returned to Prague, along with the Saxon army. The skulls of the executed lords were taken down and, according to some testimonies, were secretly buried right in Týn. According to other rumours, the remains of the Czech lords found their final resting places in the Church of St. Salvator. In any case, the skulls were never found. The souls of all twenty-seven of the executed Lords supposedly meet late at night in front of the Old Town House every year on June twenty-first, at the place of their execution, in order to watch the functioning of the horologium. If the clock works well, the souls depart again peacefully. However, if the machinery seizes up, it's a bad omen: the Czech Republic can expect a bad year. Twelve of the souls of the executed lords withdraw back to Týn church while the rest of the souls, noiselessly and with enormous grief, disappear among the meandering Old Town streets.

With the advance of re-Catholicization after the Thirty Years' War, and as a result of the fire of 1679, when the original vault of the central aisle cracked and caved in, the interior of the church acquired Baroque ornamentation in the form of a new vaulting, a hefty central alter and an organ loft, completed in approximately 1670 by Giovanni Domenico Orsini. In the organ loft, there are two of the oldest surviving Prague organs, made in the years 1670–73 by the master Mundt, from Cologne. The other seventeen altars also bear a Baroque signature, whose sculptural decorations originate primarily from the workshop of Jan Jiří

Gothic stone pulpit from the 15th century

◀ Týn organ, from the second half of the 17th century, is the oldest preserved organ in Prague.

The Baroque altar Calvary with Gothic carvings by Master of the Týn crucifixion

Bendl, and partially from masters M. V. Jäckel, Weiss and František Preiss. In the seventeenth century, the Italian master Girolamo Romani created hanging paintings entitled *The Visit of the Virgin Mary* and *Sacrificing in the Church* for the chancel of the church. In the central aisle, we can also admire a collection of statues of Christ, the Virgin Mary and the apostles, created at the end of the seventeenth century by Ottavio Mosto.

The central black-gold main altar, made in the year 1649, is adorned by statues of the Czech patrons St. Vaclav and St. Vitus, St. Ludmila, St. Vojtěch, St. Prokop, and St. Zigmund. On the highest part of the altar there is a statue of the Archangel Michael, complemented by figures of St. Peter and St. Paul. The altars are dominated by a central painting entitled *the Assumption of the Virgin Mary* by the prominent Czech Baroque artist Karel Škréta, who on account of this specific painting was accepted to the Old Town Painters' Guild. Škréta, originally Evangelical and only later converted to Catholicism„ was by chance born in close proximity to the Týn church, at 5 Týn Street. Škréta also decorated many of the other altars in the church: we can see his work in the left aisle at the altar of the Annunciation of the Virgin Mary from 1922 with a painting on the same subject, and Škréta paintings can also be found on the altar of St. Josef on the first pillar of the left aisle. On the second pillar, under the stone baldachin from the master Matěj Rejsek, there is another painting by Škréta of St. Lucas.

Originally, the grave of the bishop Lucian Augustin from Mirandola was under the baldachin. The bishop ordained Ultraquist priests in Prague from 1482. However, he soon built up a strong dislike among Prague dwellers, allegedly on account of his extreme greed. After the Battle of White Mountain, his remains were discarded and his grave was destroyed.

Another Škréta painting can be found on the fourth pillar on the altar of St. Vojtěch. In the neighbouring latticed balcony, at the front of the left aisle reminiscent of a cage, the Old Town executioner, according to legend, participated in church services. It contains, however, a small section connecting a suspended passageway with the Gothic dome at

A niche in the gable of the central nave, in which a chalice was originally placed, which, however, was after the victory of Catholicism in the Czech lands replaced by a statue of the Madonna

Altar of John the Baptist with a Renaissance carving of Christ's baptism in the middle

▶ The altarpiece of the Assumption of the Virgin Mary by Charles Škréta

the Stone bell. The passageway spans the narrow Týn street and is easily visible from the vantage point of Old Town Square. Let's return to Týn: in the left aisle, we shouldn't overlook the altar of St. Kryšpín and Krišpina from the year 1714, featuring a painting by another Baroque master, Michael Hallwach. The late Baroque altar of St. Expedite is also worth a look. Finally, we come to the concluding, top Baroque Calvary, which is complemented by a Gothic carving entitled *Calvary,* by the Master of Týn crucifixions, created before the outbreak of the Hussite wars. The last part of the left aisle is decorated by a painting of St. Nicodemus, Mary Magdalena and the apostles, painted by an unknown artist. The work dates back to the end of the seventeenth century. At the side exit on the side of the left aisle, flowing out to Týnská street, you can also see a painting of St. Joseph by J."J. Heinsch and another painting of the Preaching of St. John the Baptist by an unknown author.

Another work by the Master of Týn crucifixions, the statue of the Týn Madonna, is decorated by a neo-Gothic altar near the end of the right church aisle. Here as well – at the triumphal arch – we discover the Baroque altar of St. Barbora with another Škréta painting from the year 1660; then, at the first pillar, there is an altar with a scene of Christ on the Mount of Olives. The altar of St. John the Baptist follows, with a Renaissance carving dating back to the first half of the sixteenth century and depicting the baptism of Christ, the Sacred Mother; then, on the altar wings, the bowing of the three kings, the annunciation of the Virgin Mary, and the beheading of St. John the Baptist. The altar of St. Wenceslas from 1664 also deserves attention, dedicated to Tým's maltsters, or the altar of St. Ann from the year 1706, or the neo-Gothic altar of the Seven Sorrows of the Virgin Mary, created in the year 1880 by the painter Antonín Lhota and the carver Eduard Veselý. In the right aisle, there is also a large oval painting by Petr Brandl from the first quarter of the eighteenth century, depicting the meeting between St. Wenceslas and Emperor Henry at the Imperial Diet. Finally, we shouldn't overlook the marble sculpture of St. Cyril and Methodius, a work by the hand of Emanuel Max and finished in 1845 at a cost of ten thousand gold pieces. Placing the giant marble statue into the church space took four days and required the widening of the church gate.

In the interior we can also admire a stone pulpit from the beginning of the fifteenth century. Another interesting artifact is a tin baptismal font from the year 1414, the largest and oldest of its kind in Prague. Church visitors will also be surprised by the number of stone grave ledgers with rich relief ornamentation, exhibiting the visual signatures of the Renaissance and Baroque styles. In particular, the grave ledger of Tycho de Brahe demands one's notice, located at the first pillar on the central aisle. The court astronomer to the Emperor Rudolph II, Brahe was buried here on the fourth of November, 1601. At the end of the north aisle there is the grave ledger of a Jewish boy named Šimon Abeles from the year 1694. The fate of this young lad was tragic: when the boy was around twelve, he decided to change to the Catholic faith and thereby extract himself from an unhappy family background. The baptism, which should have been arranged by the Jesuits, never came to fruition. The boy's outraged father, Lazar Abeles, and his helper, Levi Hüsel, murdered the boy on the twenty-first of February, 1694. The father was thrown into the city jail, where he hung himself, while his co-conspirator was tortured on the breaking wheel. Despite the fact that the boy wasn't christened, the archbishop consented to Šimon being buried in the Catholic Church, so that at least in death he could find his yearned-for peace.

There is more sad history tied to Týn church. The largest and oldest church bell, called Marie, weighs in at over six tons and dates back to the sixteenth century; it was allegedly acquired from the financial donations of a certain rich and noble townswoman. Her renowned cruelty led to the death of one of her servants, but her guilty conscience led her to atonement. She gave her property away to the poor, and from that money she had the Marie bell made; in the end, she even wore a monk's attire. However, none of these things were enough to cleanse her of her sin, and so on a stormy night she came into view in the tower of Týn church, where her bell was swinging, sadly pronouncing her guilt into the darkness above the rooftops of Old Town…

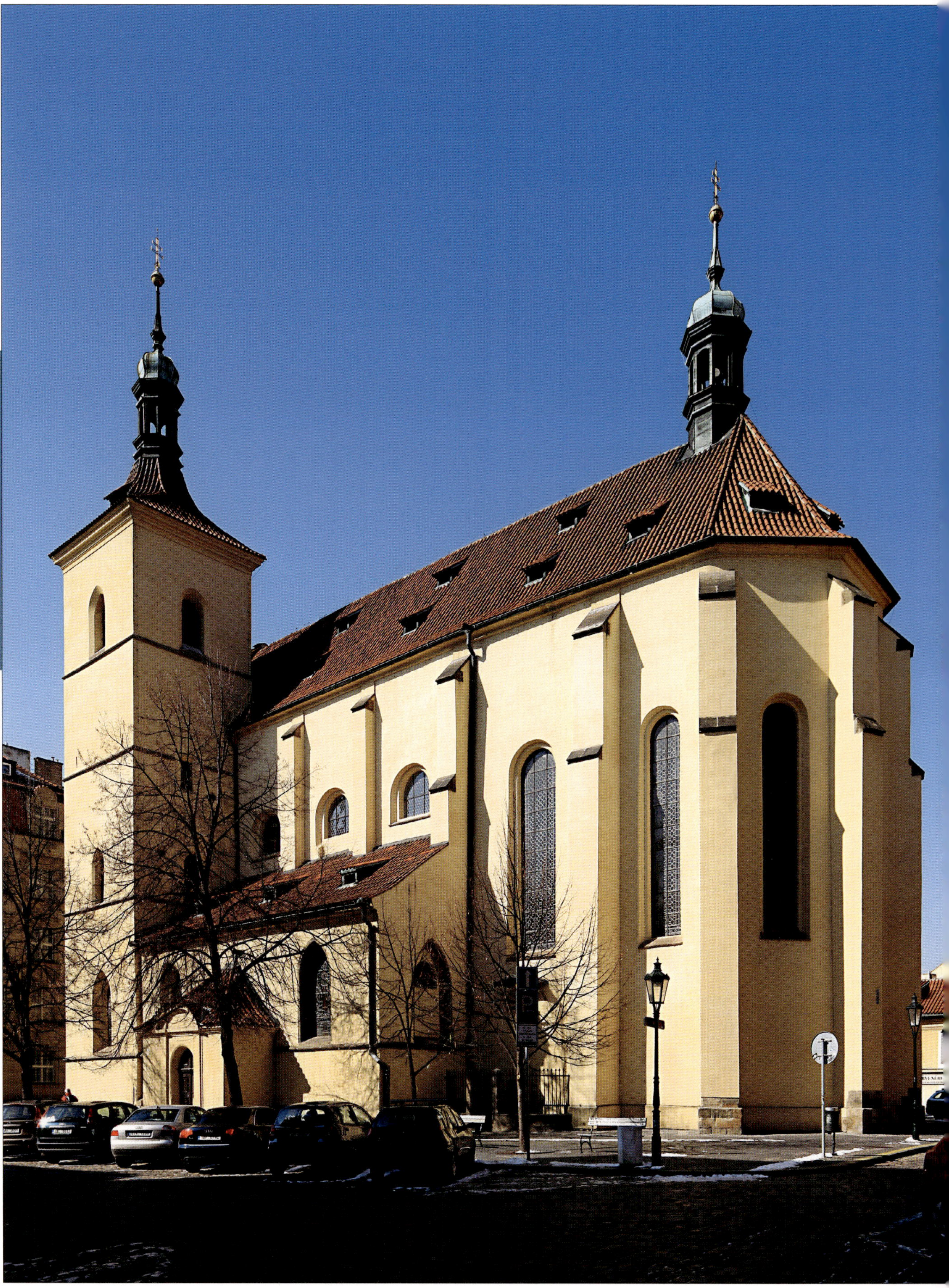

THE CHURCH OF ST. HAŠTAL

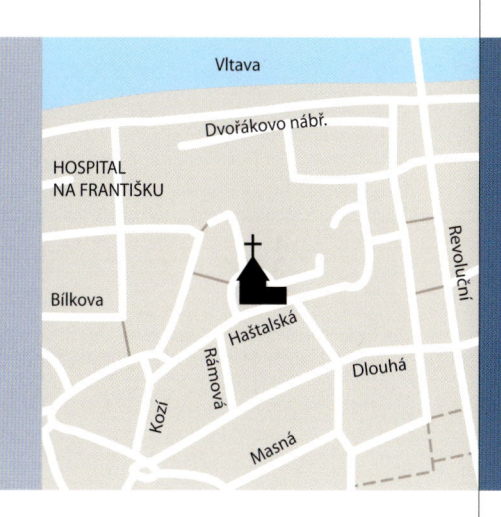

One of the most significant buildings: built in a late Gothic style and later rebuilt in a Baroque style.

Hastel Square, Prague 1 - Old Town

Transport: Metro A Staroměstská, Tram 17, 18 Staroměstská

Worship:
Sun 11:00 am (first and last Sunday of the month)

Built in 1234
1375 completed in its present form
17th century Baroque reconstruction

The Church of St. Haštal has a rich and troubled history. It is the only church in the Czech Republic dedicated to St. Haštal; in fact, in the whole of Europe there are relatively few St. Haštal churches. The name of the patron of this church is the Czech version of the Latin name Castullus. So was the name of a Roman patrician, living in the third century. Although he was the custodian of the Imperial Palace, he secretly accepted baptism along with his wife. Not only did he continue to secretly spread the Christian faith, but he also hid his fellow Christians from Diocletian's persecution, hiding them right under the Emperor's nose in the palace. After being discovered, Castullus was tortured and finally executed in the year 287.

On the site of today's St. Haštal church, there was originally another building - evidently also dedicated to St. Haštal -, a Romanesque church, built approximately in the middle of the twelfth century. The first written information about this sanctuary can be found in the deeds of King Vaclav I, from the year 1234. In the 1440s, the foundation of a Gothic, three-aisle basilica was laid on the site of the old Romanesque church, and its construction took almost thirty years. However, the original design was abandoned, and instead of a three-aisle basilica, a two-aisle church with

Gargoyle under the supporting ribs of the northern two-nave hall

Statue of the Calvary by the school of F. M. Brokoff

an All Saints chapel was built. The sanctuary was completed before the year 1375.

The next century wasn't very peaceful for The Church of St. Haštal. In the year 1420 it was occupied by Hussites, who compelled Communion under both the blood and the body of Christ for laymen, and that practice was preserved for the next two centuries. About twelve years later, in the year 1432, Old Town was hit by a flood; the church was completely inundated, and expensive repairs were needed. Nevertheless, the reconstruction of the church successfully continued and the altars were able to be consecrated again in the year 1436.

Contemporary sources allege that a school also belonged to the church. However, in the first half of the sixteenth century, it had such a bad reputation that a derisive ditty circulated among Prague people at the time: "St. Haštal – a school just like a jail cell!" In order to build a new school, the parishioners had to sell a part of the church's property, specifically eighteen silver chalices and one monstrance. While this method may seem surprising, it bore fruit and the parishioners were able to start building new school buildings in the year 1620.

Two years later, the Church of St. Haštal cancelled the right to administer under both methods. Only a couple of decades later, the church was completely destroyed during the massive Old Town blaze, started by agents of the French King. The fire, which occurred on June twenty-first, 1689, destroyed the tower and the main space of the temple; its vault split open in the heat and crashed to the ground. The heat was allegedly so hot that even the church bell melted. Only the side aisle escaped the hellish fire, by which the original Gothic shape survived; today's visitors can still take delight from the ribbed vault, the great architectural work of the Luxembourg Gothics. The sacristy also remained untouched, which had been consecrated in the year 1375 and decorated with Gothic frescoes depicting Christ's last supper and the crucifixion, as well as the heads of the apostles.

The repairs following the fire lasted almost to the conclusion of the seventeenth century and the church acquired a new Baroque vault, a new chancel and frontal gable. In

General view into the main nave with the altar and pulpit

Close up of the Calvary statue by the school of F. M. Brokoff

1731, the altar was also rebuilt in a Gothic style, but in 1883 it acquired a neo-Renaissance design from the architect Antonín Baum. A glassed-in compartment is situated on the central altar, intended for the relics of Haštal. It is interesting to note that the Old Town dogcatchers also had their own altar, catching wandering dogs and cats.

In the same year, the church was decorated with statues of John of Nepomuk and St. John the Baptist, the last works by the master F. M. Brokoff, who died that year. From his workshop we can also find *Calvary* from the year 1716. We can also admire here the Baroque painting *Christ in the Garden of Gethsemane*, dating back to the year 1700, which can be found on the north wall of the presbytery. We should also take note of the pulpit from 1730, adorned with reliefs depicting the Baptism of Christ, the four Evangelists, and the imprisonment of St. Haštal, as well as sculptures of Christ the Saviour, Moses and St. Gregorius.

In the end, in spite of a series of mishaps, the church of St. Haštal was fortunate in that, unlike a whole range of other churches, it wasn't affected by Joseph's reforms. However, the adjacent cemetery wasn't so lucky, where the deceased were placed until 1784. In the end, the cemetery was destroyed in the year 1832 and the exhumed remains were transported to the largest cemetery in Prague, Olšany. House No. 1041, which in the past served as a mortuary, serves as a reminder of the former final resting place…

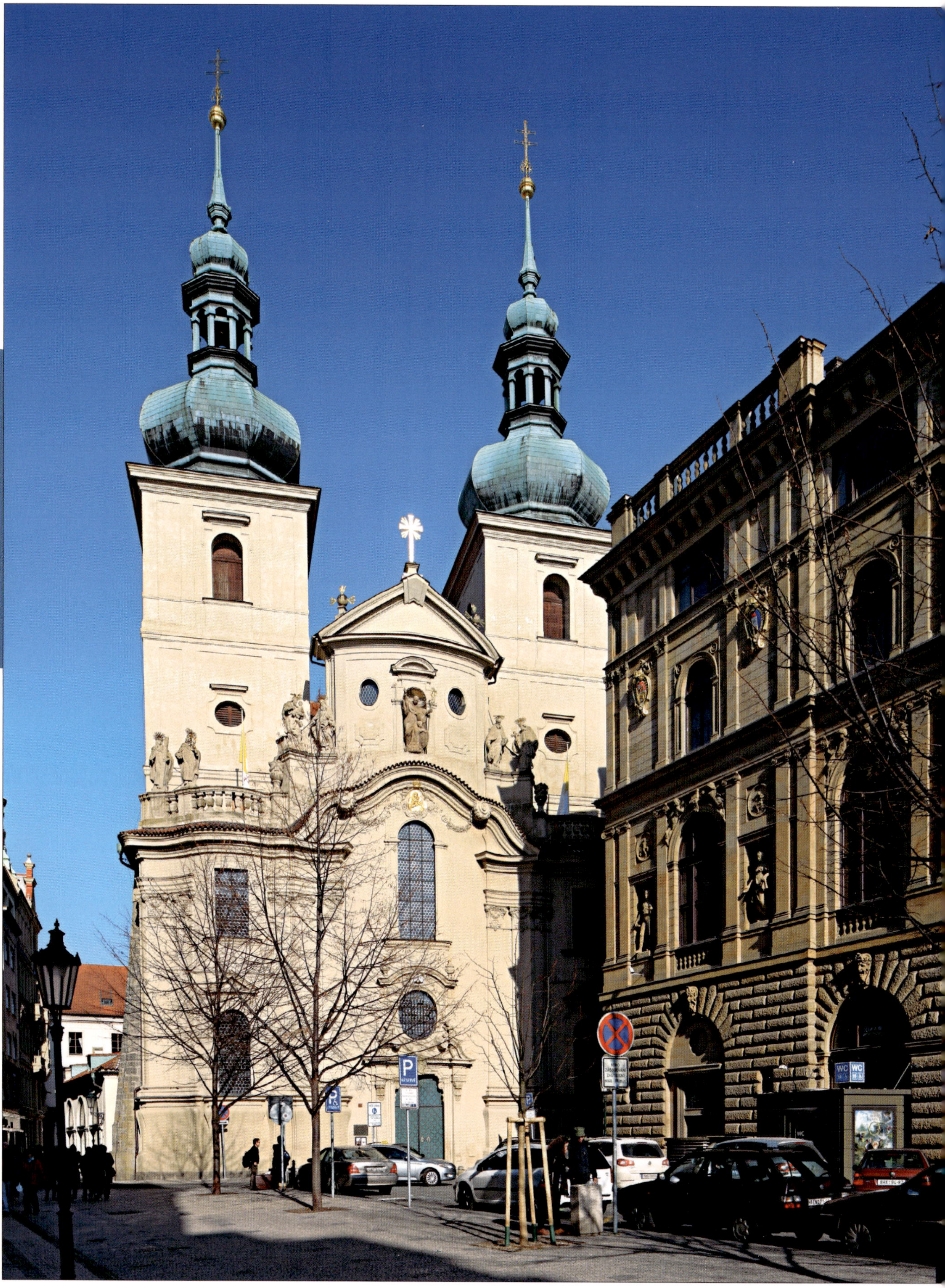
P
WC WC

THE CHURCH OF ST. HAVEL

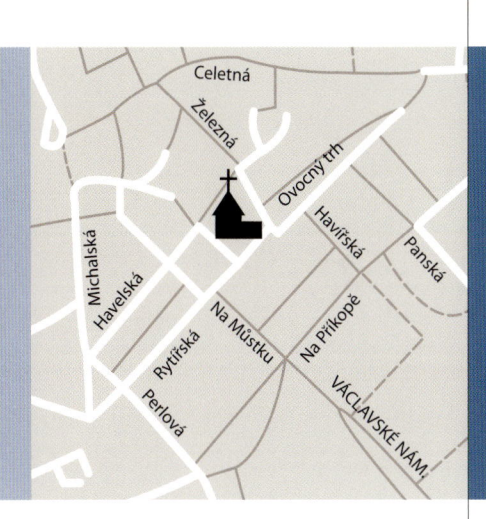

A massive Baroque church with opulent, artistic ornamentation, built on the basis of a Gothic, three-aisle Basilica.

Havelská st., Prague 1 - Old Town
Transport: Metro A/B Můstek
Worship:
Mon-Fri 12:30 pm (apart from July and August), Sun 8:30 am

1232 founded
14th century - rebuilt in Gothic style
17th century - redone in a Baroque style
18th century - completion of the western facade

In the first half of the thirteenth century the space around today's Havelské marketplace was on the periphery of Old Town buildings. This space was later to be built up, following a decision by Wenceslas I in the 1330s. The central point of the newly built site was to become a large marketplace, facing the heart of Old Town on one side and sealed by a fortification system on the other side, leading in an arc from the Vltava, across today's Revoluční street, Na Příkopě street and Národní, back to the bank of the Vltava. Old Town thereby acquired its first bulwark of fortification. The main building in the new marketplace became the Romanesque Church of St. Havel.

A short time later, the small church was given the name of the whole newly built space, before it merged with Old Town: *Civitas circa S. Gallum*, Havel Town. During the course of the fourteenth century, the church was rebuilt into a three-aisle, supreme Gothic basilica with two towers in the facade. It's interesting to note that the left tower is made of stone while the right is built from brick. From the Gothic form of St. Havel's church, only the foundation of the west tower, the arcade in the chancel, and some minute architectural elements have survived to the present day. The temple, in its new Gothic style, was given the skull of the Irish monk St. Havel, acquired from the Swiss monas-

Close up of a Crying St. Mary Magdalena from the Calvary Chapel

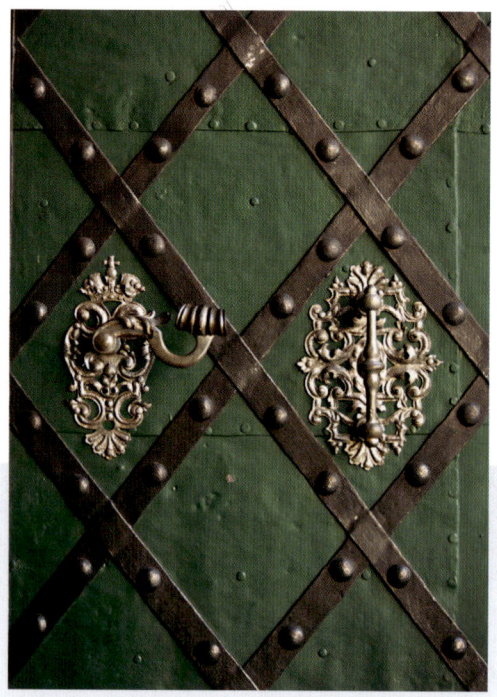

Close up of the gate

▶ Statues of the Calvary by F. M. Brokoff

tery of St. Gallen by Charles IV, a collector of relics. In the second part of the fourteenth century, the Church of St. Havel became a preaching site for the predecessors of the Hussites, primarily the German Augustinian priest Konrad Waldhauser; he came to the church at the invitation of Charles IV between the years 1358-60, to speak about the necessity of Church reforms. Jan Milíč from Kroměříž was another preacher at the church during this time. In the years 1380-90, the custodian of St. Havel's Church became another prominent personality in Czech spiritual and cultural history; this was actually the Imperial and Archepiscopal notary John of Nepomuk. Around the year 1404, Jan Hus preached against the inequity of the Church inside the very walls of the church. It could be expected that the Church of St. Havel would be among the first to go over to the side of the Calixtines from the beginning of the Hussite storm, and it is necessary to acknowledge here that therefore – unlike a whole range of other church buildings and sanctuaries – it was protected and didn't suffer any damage. The church belonged to the grouping of churches which was consecrated with the acceptance of church service under both methods.

Changes came about after the Battle of White Mountain, which signified a repeated re-Catholicization of the Czech territory. In the year 1621, the Old Town councilman Jan Kutnauer was buried in the cellar space of St. Havel's church. He was one of the twenty-seven Bohemian lords which were executed in Old Town Square after the Battle of White Mountain.

Religious tolerance had existed to a significant extent up until this point; however, it ended decisively with the defeat of the Bohemian Protestants at the Battle of White Mountain. One result was the decision In 1627 by Emperor Ferdinand IIto issue the Church of St. Havel to the Order of the Shoe-wearing Carmelites. It is, however, necessary to add that the parish of St. Havel was at that time abandoned, the last of the Ultraquists having fled the parish back in 1621. From the year 1624 up until the decree of Ferdinand II, the church was under the administration of the Polish Carmelite clergymen. The first Shoe-wearing

Carmelites, whose rule was characterized more for its moderate monasticism than that of the Barefoot Carmelites, were thereafter Polish monks who for almost fifty years had been trying to purchase land and buildings around the church from the Old Town townsmen, so that they could build a monastery. They finally succeeded in the year 1671, when construction was initiated; it wasn't finished until 1704. Today we can find the monastery buildings on the back tract of the St. Havel temple.

On the cusp of the eighteenth century, the Church of St. Havel underwent a Baroque reconstruction under the leadership of Giovanni Domenico Orsi and Pavel Ignác Bayer. However, the reconstruction wasn't entirely thorough, and so it is possible to find architectural and building elements of the original medieval basilica, primarily in the interior.

Not only is the history of the St. Havel Church rich and interesting, but its interior decoration definitely is as well. In the main aisle, beneath the Gothic vault, we can't overlook the Baroque portal altar with statues of the Holy Trinity, the Crucifixion, and the Lamb of God all made by the sculptor M. V. Jäckel around 1725. Older than these statues, of course, is the central altar paintings depicting the Virgin Mary and the Carmelite order of saints, with St. Havel in the center; in the lower part there is a canvas of Emperor Leopold I with his wife and children. The painting was created in approximately 1696 by the master Jan Kryštof Liška from Rottenwald. To the right of the central altar, we find three side altars: the altar of the Virgin Mary, the altar of John the Baptist and finally the altar of St. Barbora. We should also point out that in the altar of the Virgin Mary there is a large Baroque painting depicting the appearance of Mary to the prophet Eliaš, as well as statues of Jindřich and Leopold. The altar of John the Baptist is complemented by statues of Peter and Paul and a painting of the Baptism of Christ, and the altar of St. Barbora is decorated with statues of St. Catherine and St. Markéta together with an interpretation of the beheading of St. Barbora. On the opposite side of the temple aisle, there is the altar of St. Albert, a Sicilian saint from the thirteenth century. Next to that is the altar of St. Theresa from Ávila and Mary

Statues of saints on the main façade by F. M. Jäckel form early 18th Century

▶ Calvary chapel

Magdalene de Pazzi. Around the painting depicting the two saints exiting a gloomy church, there are statues of St. Albert and St. Anastasius from Persia. We finish our tour of the St. Havel altars at the altar of St. Ann, with a depiction of this saint at the side of St. Joseph and the Virgin Mary.

From the main aisle we can set out for the two sides, in each of which a chapel is built. In the left aisle we can stop in front of the Chapel of St. Wenceslas from the year 1730, which is also named the Calvary Chapel; its sculptural ornamentation – depicting the Four Evangelists – is one of the most successful works from the artist F. M. Brokoff. Behind the Calvary statue, we can see a wall mural from the same period, depicting the crucifixion of the two rogues, the bearing of the cross, and finally the Final Judgement of the Saviour. In the right aisle, we find two chapels: the lower one is known as Carmel, with a Baroque altar and statues of St. Šimon Stock and St. John the Baptist from J. A. Quittainer; the upper one is the so-called Imperial altar, which is situated in the floor above the Carmel chapel. The Carmel chapel was built in the year 1671 and the Our Lady of Mt. Carmel altar painting probably comes from the same period. The chapel is opulently ornamented by the stucco work of G. B. Comet as well as the grave of Karel Škréta, Czech Baroque painter from the seventeenth century. It is said that Škréta is actually the creator of the altar painting *Our Lady of Mt. Carmel*, for whose rendering his sweetheart was the inspiration.

Of course, the massive three-aisle building is also remarkable when viewed from the outside. At first glance, one's attention is captured by the dynamic, Baroque waved ledging which rises up the church's facade with a certain heaviness. Along the side of its gable stand eight statues from the aforementioned M. V. Jäckel, probably created in the years 1725-27. A massive Baroque bell looms from both sides of the central aisle façade, in which the remains of the original Gothic windows are preserved in some places. Under the church there is also a labyrinth of corridors, catacombs and crypts, which are unfortunately currently inaccessible.

69

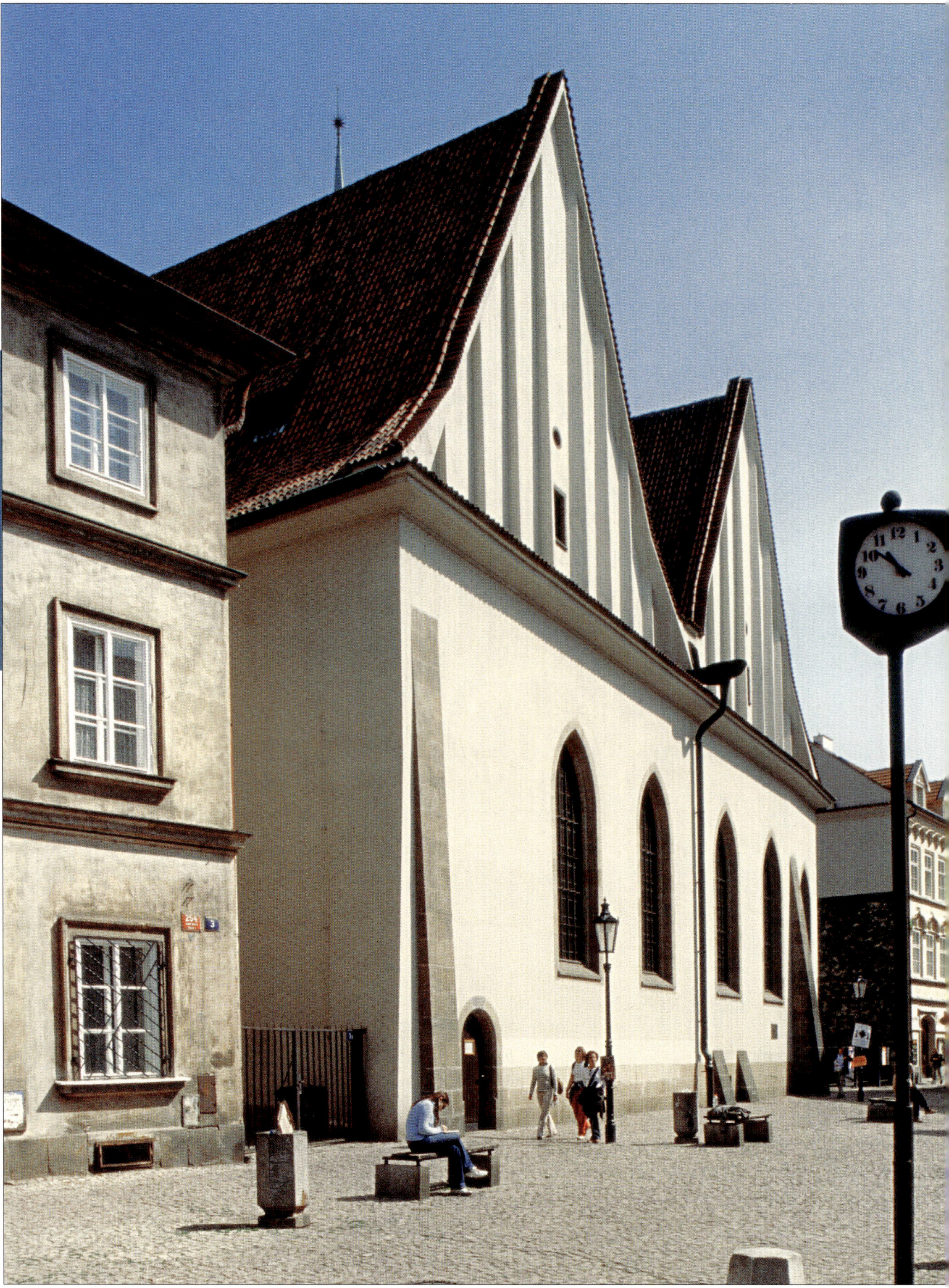

BETHLEHEM CHAPEL

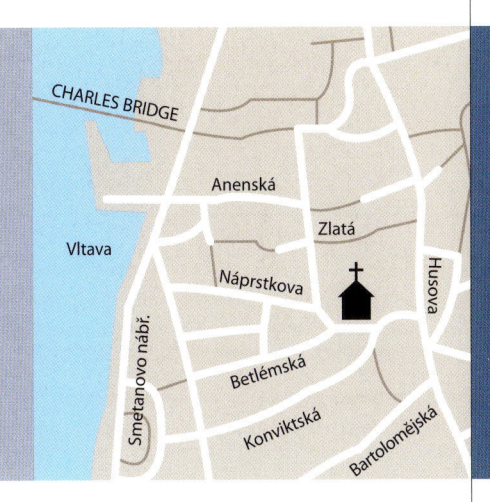

A reconstructed chapel dating from the end of the fourteenth century, which became the preaching center of Jan Hus, a reformer of the Catholic church. After he was burned at the stake on the sixth of July, 1415, the chapel became a symbolic spiritual place for the Hussites.

Bethlehem Square255/4, Prague 1 - Old Town
Transport: Metro A/B Můstek, Tram 17, 18 Karlovy lázně, 6, 9, 18, 22 Národní třída
Worship: none
Built in 1391-1394
1786 destroyed
1950-1952 copy built

If one sets out from the extensive Baroque Clementine complex via the narrow, crooked and eternally damp Liliová street and heads in the direction of the former Old Town fortification wall, they will have to go through a miniature sqaure named Bethlehem Square, wedged between Betlémská, Konviktská and Husova streets. The pair of tall, sharp and bent gables of Bethlehem Chapel will then capture the visitor's attention.

The chapel was built in the years 1391-1394 as a sanctuary for preaching in Czech, the native language. The foundation was placed partially in the cross-shaped garden and partially in the cemetery belonging to the Romanesque, later Gothic-restyled Church of St. Phillip and St. Jacob, whose origin can be traced to around the year 1100. That church was eventually torn down. According to the surviving historical lists, it is possible to determine that it was built almost two meters from the location of the chapel façade today, which was actually enclosed on all sides. In light of the fact that its location was literally in the middle of the medieval city, the building was forced to adapt architecturally along with the evolving spatial possibilities, and the chapel thereby acquired its peculiar, trapezoidal floor plan.

The chapel primarily became historically significant on account of Jan Hus, who became its curator on the 14th of

Among the murals can be found, among other things, musical notations from the Jistebniz Hymn Book, a collection of spiritual songs of the 15th century, in which there are also Hussite songs written.

March, 1402. Hus's preaching, which took place here up until February 1413, and in which he strove for the reformation of the Catholic Church, protested against the selling of indulgences for the war of Pope John XXIII with the Neapolitan King and preached for a return to the Apostolic Church; his sermons drew believes from both Prague and the wider surrounding area to his chapel. Hus's performance, which made Bethlehem a center for Czech reformist tendencies, initiated an anti-Church storm, which exploded into a protracted religious war after Hus was burned at the stake in Konstanz on the 6th of July, 1415. The chapel was not originally intended for any other purpose than preaching, and wasn't designated for celebrating the Eucharist; however, after an interdict had been pronounced over Hus and while he was imprisoned in Konstanz, church services were also given in the chapel, of course with the acceptance of both methods (*sub utraque specie*), which was one of the reform requirements of Hus's supporters. Hus had also taught at Prague University since 1398, and became its rector between 1409 and 1410; for this reason, Bethlehem Chapel wasn't connected only with believers, but also with Prague's intellectuals and with the University.

At the end of the Middle Ages and during the whole of the sixteenth century, the chapel was used as an ordinary parish church. In spite of the fact that references to Hussites were slowly being repressed on account of the re-Catholicization efforts, Jan Hus continued to be identified with the Bethlehem Chapel, even in the official documents of Emperor Rudolph II, who had the chapel renewed in 1548. In the same year, the chapel was also rebuilt and probably acquired its late Gothic, netted, ribbed vaulting at that time. Afterwards, care of the chapel was taken over by the Bohemian Brethren, linked to the Hussite legacy to a certain extent. Prague University also fell under Jesuit administration. At the beginning of the eighteenth century, the chapel gained its Baroque sculptural ornamentation from Matyáš Bernard Braun. When the order granting the chapel to the Jesuits was cancelled in 1773, the chapel was handed over to the parish church of St. Jiljí as its branch

The neo-Gothic windows let light into the well, which was in the open before the building of Bethlehem Chapel. When a copy of the chapel was being built, the well was restored.

Renewed pulpit and the original stone jambs of doors and windows

sanctuary. Nevertheless, the chapel had gone into disrepair over a long period, and so before long, in 1786, it was demolished. For almost 50 years the freed-up space on Bethlehem square served as a place to store wood. It was only in 1836 that a three-storey, classicistic rental apartment building was built there. It seemed that Bethlehem Chapel had finally been wiped off the map of Prague's religious historical sites for good. However, in 1919, a year after the pronouncement of an independent Czechoslovakia an isolated archeological survey indicated that the original Gothic masonry and foundation of the chapel remained in existence. After the Communist takeover in the year 1948, the intruding apartment building was demolished, and the renewal of the chapel was carried out.

It is, however, necessary to point out that ideological reasons prevailed more in this decision than cultural or historical ones. Communist propaganda misinterpreted Hus's opinions and those of the Hussite group, comprised primarily of radical villagers, intellectuals, and Czech nobility; they portrayed Hussites as an archetype of the later proletariat, struggling against the Church, the nobility, and wealthy townspeople. The renovation of the chapel was taken over by renowned architect Jaroslav Fragner; the reconstruction, which was carried out between the years 1950–52, also covered the foundation of the older St. Phillip and St. Jacob Church. Today's incarnation of the chapel copies the original trapezoidal floor plan. The inside of the space is enclosed by wooden ceilings, under which, in the western wall, there are wooden choir lofts for singers and musicians. Five neo-Gothic refracted windows illuminate a wall mural depicting the events of the Council of Constance, copying the illustrations from the Jena Codex, from the Reichenthal Chronicles, the musical score of the Hussite song from the Jistebník hymn book, or the Ten Commandments. In the abutting, so-called Vicar house, which in the past served as a vicarage, is a small museum of the master, Jan Hus.

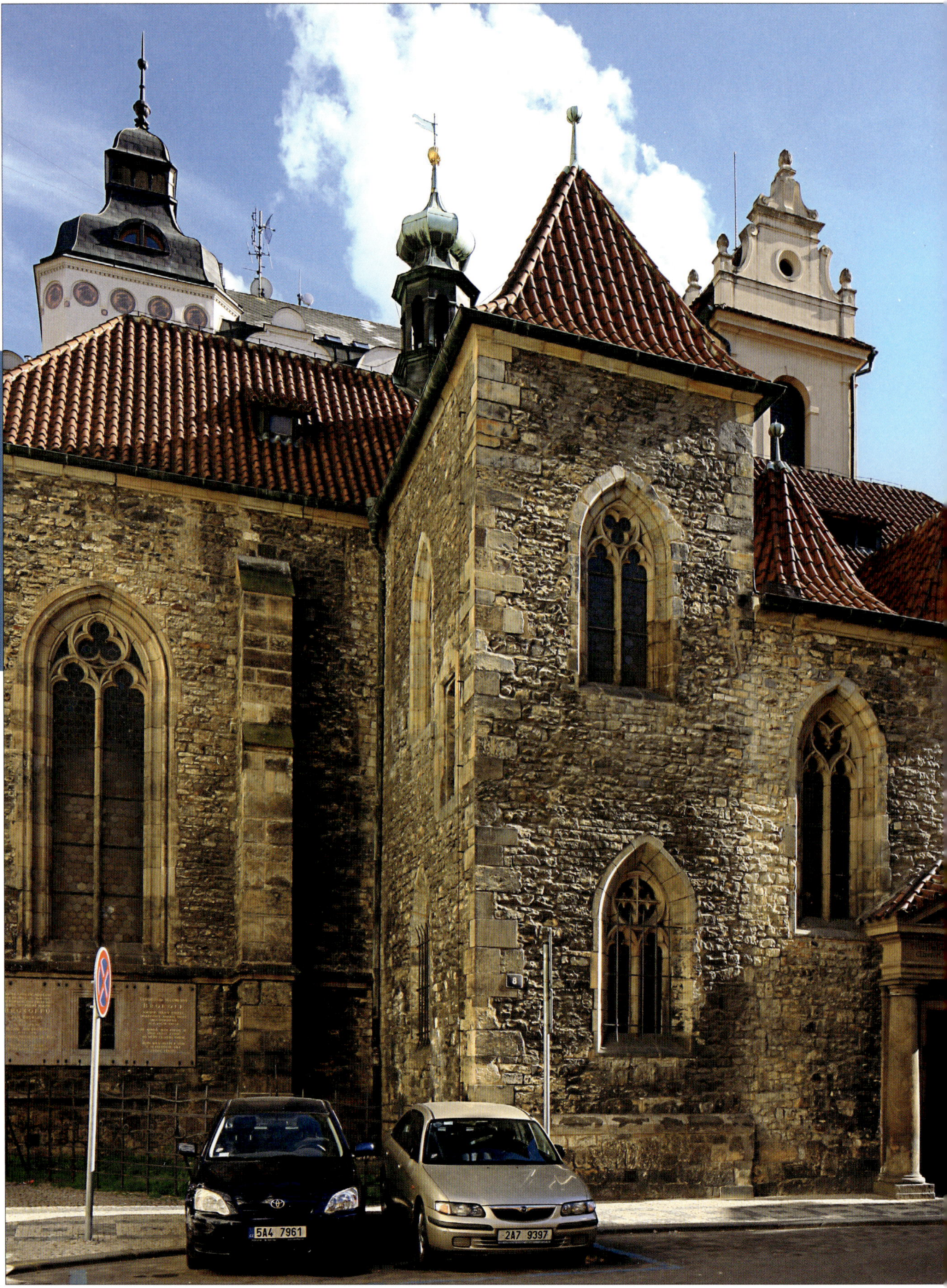
5A4 7961
2A7 9397

ST. MARTIN IN THE WALL CHURCH

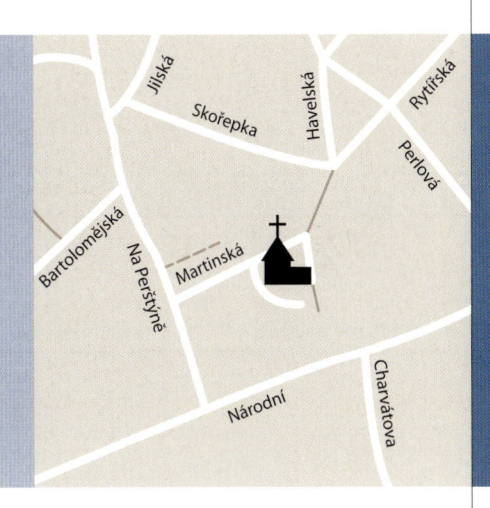

A noteworthy and mysterious Gothic church with a Romanesque foundation in the middle of modern city buildings, one of Prague's most significant spiritual and cultural sites from the late Middle Ages.

Martinská 8, Prague 1 - Old Town

Transport: Metro A/B Můstek, Tram 6, 9, 18, 22 Národní třída

Worship:
Sun 7:30 pm

Built in 1178-1187
1360-1370 Gothic reconstruction
1488 late Gothic construction completed
1784 closed
1905-1906 restored
1919 passed on to the Evangelical Church of the Czech Brethren

St. Martin in the Wall Church is sure to take visitors off guard. If we set off from Národní Street, which in the thirteenth century passed through the first Prague fortification, or if we approach St. Martin's Church from the Uhelný marketplace, the black, hefty walls of the church always emerge in front of you unexpectedly. Today, the church stands on a tiny parcel of land, enclosed on all four sides by tall townhouse buildings. From the Uhelný marketplace, a small, winding street leads to the church, and from Národní Street we can reach it via a short passageway behind the church.

On the site of St. Martin's Church, in the first half of the twelfth century, was one of Prague's oldest settlements, called St. Martin's Manor. The sanctuary of St. Martin was built here between 1178-87. In the first half of the thirteenth century the south wall was originally a Romanesque church with architectural elements of a basilica incorporated into a bulwark wall, which is how the sanctuary acquired its nickname "in the wall". The construction of a fortification system divided the St. Martin settlement into two separate parts: the first - with St. Martin Church - was merged with the emerging Havel Town; the second, which found itself behind the bulwark, formed the foundation of the later New Town, which Charles IV commenced building in the middle of the fourteenth century.

The austere decor and absence of an altar corresponds to the use of the church by the Protestant Church of the Czech brethren

View of the interior from the pulpit and communion table

In the second half of the fourteenth century, under the reign of Charles IV, the church acquired a Gothic form. The height of the aisle of the church was raised and it received a new vaulting. In addition, a massive, prismatic wall was added in the southwest corner, which is still visible today. In the years 1360–70 it acquired a presbytery, which added a ribbed vault and expanded the interior of the church. The Gothic reconstruction was completed in 1488, and so St. Martin's Church contains architectural elements of Romanesque style as well as elements of upper and late Gothic styles. The church entered the history of late medieval Prague in the year 1414; it was here, at the impulse of Jacob of Stříbro, that the priest Jan of Hradec began to serve communion under both methods, both the blood and the body, to lords and laypersons for the first time. St. Martin's church remained joined with the Hussites. In the year 1433, the Hussites organized an Assembly of St. Martin, which should have passed a resolution for blockading the Catholic Plzen, but also opened up space for negotiations with the Catholics. The radical wing of the Hussite movement was thereby weakened. St. Martin's church survived a dramatic event in the fifteenth century – the Hussite wars –, but then fate caught up with it in 1678 when it caught fire. During the subsequent renovation of the church, the upper part of the tower in particular had to be rebuilt, and it acquired its current form which is distinctive at first sight. Another calamity struck the church in the year 1787, when it was shut down on account of Joseph's reforms. For the following decade, it served primarily as a storage site, and living spaces were later built inside of it as well. Only at the beginning of the nineteenth century was the church, renewed in accordance with plans by the architect Kamil Hilbert. Archaeological research subsequently uncovered the original Romanesque masonry work and the torso of the Romanesque sanctuary. Today, St. Martin in the Wall Church again functions as a place for church services under the administration of the Czech Brethren Evangelical church, and also as a beautiful, slightly sombre arena for chamber concerts.

There is also a nice legend connected with St. Martin's Church concerning the petrification of a boy on the roof: in

Stone gargoyle, according to legend, of a petrified boy …

times of old, a small house had been built near the church, which was widely referred to by its nickname, the Nursery. One day a woman, the widow of a Prague townsman, and her son moved into this house. Her late husband's money soon gone, the mother had no other choice but to try and earn some money as a cleaning lady. Her son stayed home and, as is usually the case, took advantage of his mother's absence and got up to all kinds of monkey business and mischief.

It wasn't enough for him to use a rope to steal apples at the marketplace, or to climb to dangerous heights on Old Town rooftops and spit on day labourers and housemaids hurrying off to the shops to take care of this or that: he needed a new perch, and so one day he decided to climb up on the ancient, bent roof of St. Martin's Church. The thing is, that right when he clambered up there, his mother was returning home. When she saw how her son was jumping around on the roof of one of God's temples, she couldn't restrain herself and she yelled furiously at up at him, "You rascal, may you turn into stone right now for your sins!" Before she even fully realized what she had said, her boy had been paralyzed in a spine-chilling pose, his body contorted, his face frozen in a terrible mask, fossilized by sin, his tongue stuck out through his half-opened mouth, as if he wanted to speak, perhaps to pray or repent, but hadn't managed to get the words out in time... His horrified mother called out to God to no avail; in vain she begged the Mother Mary. She knelt for long hours under the dark vault of the church in prayer, raising her hands in the flickering glow of the candlelight, until she was exhausted... to no avail. The boy remained turned to stone from her curse. For those who don't believe, they should go and have a look on a windy night at St. Martin in the Wall Church, and up on the roof they'll see a gargoyle in the form of a young boy.

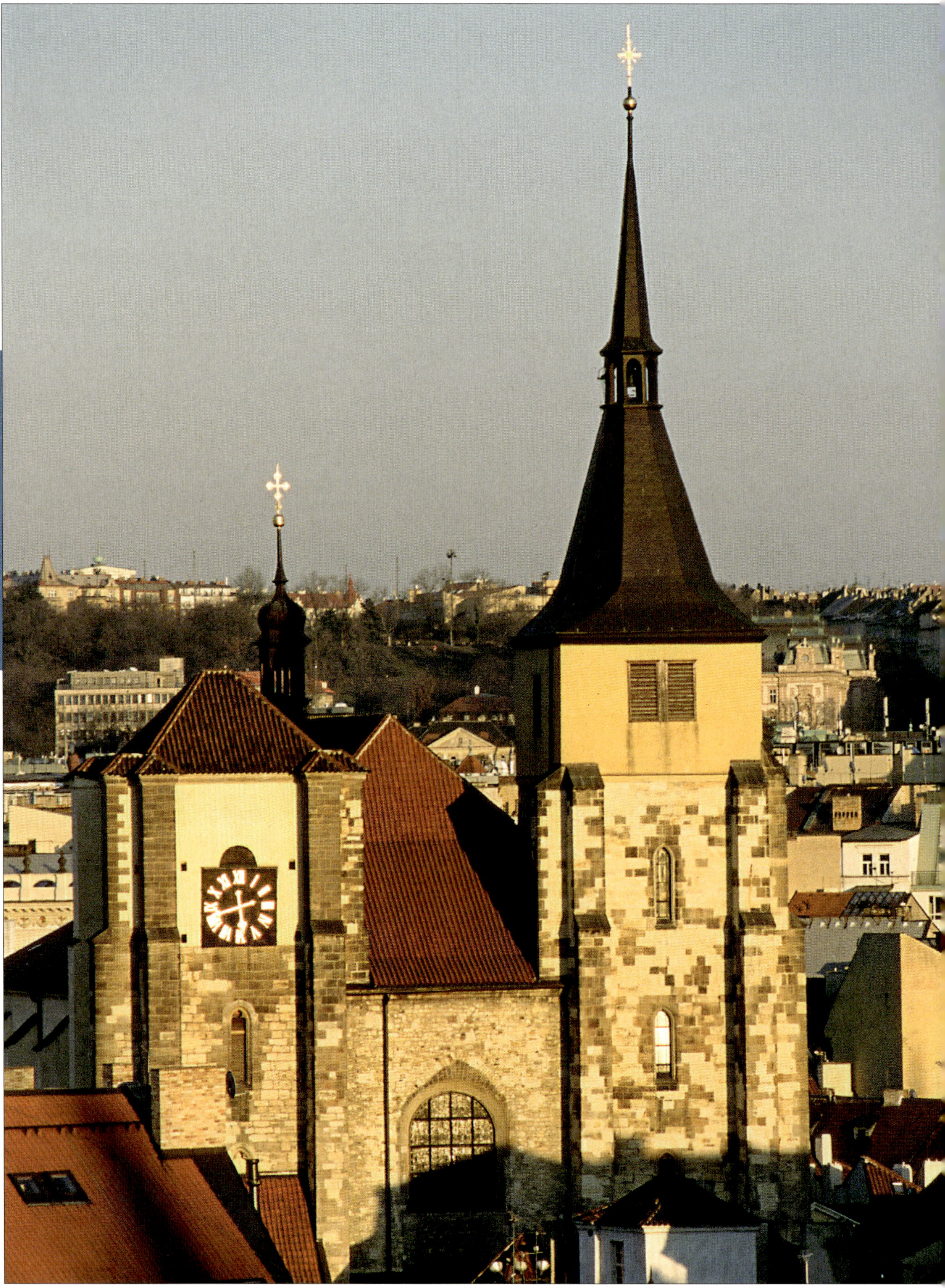

CHURCH OF ST. JILJÍ

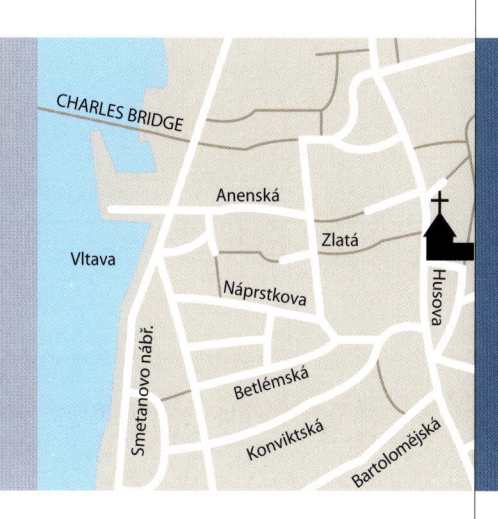

A massive Gothic temple, serving as an example of a Luxembourg Gothic structure with opulent Baroque sculptural and painting ornamentation

Husova 234/8, Prague 1 - Old Town
Transport: Metro A/B Můstek, Tram 6, 9, 18, 22 Národní třída
Worship:
Mon-Fri 7:00 am and 6:30 pm, Sat 6:30 pm, Sun 8:15 am, 9:30 am, 6:30 pm

1379 consecrated
1420 - Utraquist, demise of the chapter
1626 donated to the Dominicans
1731 Baroque reconstruction

The Church of St. Jiljí in the heart of Old Town bears the name of a remarkable saint, who had a whole range of characteristics consistent with the first Czech hermit, St. Ivan. Just like St. Ivan, St. Jiljí (Aegidius) lived a hermit's life deep in the forest, accompanied by a tame doe. The doe once caught the attention of the Visigothic King, Flavius Vamba, who was hunting. When the doe disappeared into the thicket, the angry King fired a few arrows. When he was exploring the thicket he spotted the injured hermit, embracing his doe. On the site where St. Jiljí was shot, the King had a monastery built, in which Jiljí became the first abbot. The popularity of this Saint was enormous, so it's no wonder that one of Prague's most meaningful temples was dedicated to him.

On the site of the current church, under the reign of Vaclav I, a friendly chapter of the Order of Teutonic Knights was set up at a Romanesque church. According to contemporary sources, the church was already dedicated to St. Jiljí back then. However, the chapter expanded and the church soon ceased to be suitable. In the year 1301, a well-educated member of the St. Jiljí chapter ascended to the head of the Prague Bishop's Table, Jan IV of Dražice, who decided to build a large, brand new temple for the chapter. However, coming up with the money wasn't so easy, so the

View of the main altar and side altar of St. Thomas Aquinas

▶ Altar of Our Lady of the Rosary with sculptures of St. Augustine and St. Francis of Assisi

founding stone wasn't laid until the year 1339 when John of Luxembourg occupied the Czech throne.

Although construction had begun, it progressed very slowly. The consecration of the temple finally occurred in the year 1371. Before the church was consecrated, Jan Milíč of Kroměříž, a canon and former undersecretary to Charles IV, preached there in the years 1364 to 1370. Milíč's preaching was so distinctive and effusive that in the end he was charged with spreading heresy and had to defend himself in Rome before the Pope, Urban V. Initially, he was imprisoned so that he could be quickly fired, but in the end returned to Prague with great tribute.

The Church of St. Jiljí is a beautiful specimen of the so-called Luxembourg Gothic style, deviating from basilica type Gothic sacral buildings. Unlike basilicas, St. Jiljí has as an auricular space arrangement; its three aisles are the same height and the ratio between its length and height is harmonized. The church portal is designed as an open Gothic vestibule at the top of a short staircase. Tall, four-sided Gothic towers protrude on each side of the portal, complemented by massive supporting pillars. The portal's overall design, makes for a peculiar sight on the narrow, winding Husovy Street. Visitors walking along the street by the modern colossal city buildings don't expect the sacral building; it appears as if inadvertently. In addition, the small amount of space on Husova Street doesn't allow for a complete view encompassing the façade of the church. It's only from a certain distance, from the corner of Husovy and Zlaté, that the grandeur of the entire building comes into light.

In the year 1420, the Church of St. Jiljí was occupied by Hussites. The chapter ceased to exist and the church remained Ultraquist for two centuries. That definitely saved it from the looting which occurred to a whole range of Catholic churches and monasteries. Its new Ultraquist identity also clearly played a role in these troubled times because one of the first Ultraquist vicars here was Jan of Příbram, a deliberate, calm, and restrained man in word and deed.

In the summer of 1432, lightning struck the church. During the ensuing fire the roof frame burned down com-

81

One of four Rococo confessionals from the workshop of Richard J. Prachner (1755-1760)

Close up of the main altar

pletely, the heat caused the bell to crack open, and, according to archival sources, a woman right in the middle of burying her drowned husband was also killed in the disaster. Traces of the fire are visible even today, on the north tower of the church.. The last floor of the tower was never completed, and, what's more, the design of the roof – in comparison with the south tower – is clearly an emergency solution, which in the end became permanent.

The Church of St. Jiljí was handed over to the Dominicans after the Battle of White Mountain and the ensuing re-Catholicization, following a decree by Emperor Ferdinand II. The Dominicans operated in the Czech Kingdom beginning in 1225, ten years after the establishment of their Order. After the Hussite Wars, part of the brotherhood fled, and those who didn't manage to do so in time or simply didn't succeed were killed. The Dominicans slowly began returning to the Czech region at the end of the fifteenth century; however, at that time their Order was comprised mostly of friars from Italy who didn't enjoy a very good reputation in the Czech territory, due largely to their role in the Inquisition. In the year 1555, the Prague Dominican Order totaled three friars altogether. In 1625 they moved to the Church of St. Jiljí, which at that time was in a sorry state and threatening to collapse. The first attempt at repairing the crumbling church in 1730 was more of a symbolic, cosmetic character. A more significant reconstruction was carried out three years later.

The church's reconstruction was taken charge of by the builder František Špaček with the assistance of František Maxmilián Kaňka. The reconstruction preserved the Gothic exterior, though the portal on the south side wall received Baroque plastering which covered up the original Gothic ornaments. However, the original Gothic decorations were restored in 1968. The Dominican Order remained at the church until 1950, when the church and the adjacent monastery were attacked by the Communist Committee for State Security and the friars were violently removed. Only in 1990 could the Dominicans again return to the Church of St. Jiljí.

Now, let's take a look at the interior of the three-aisle church, which also underwent a reconstruction in the

Ceiling fresco of the north aisle with scenes (top to bottom): St. Thomas teaches the Dominicans in the presence of St. Peter and Paul; St. Thomas sacrifices to the Crucified Christ his writings; St. Thomas as an infant swallows an Angelic salutation.

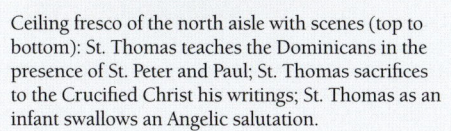

A ceiling fresco depicting the preaching of St. Dominic and St. Francis to the heretics by V. V. Rainer

eighteenth century. The Gothic vault was replaced by a new one; nevertheless, the original spacious design was retained to the greatest possible extent, in spite of the fact that its decor is pure Baroque. Visitors will definitely notice a monumental frescoe on the vault, made by the master Václav Vavřinec Reiner on the cusp of the eighteenth century. First of all, above the chancel we can see a depiction of St. Jiljí with the Visigothic king. The most expansive frescoe in the central aisle shows a scene in which St. Dominic and St. Thomas Aquinas preach to heretics. The frescoes on the vaulting of the south aisle show scenes from the life of St. Dominic, such as his meeting with St. Francis, who inspired the creation of the Dominican Friars with his emphasis on intuition and emotional cognition consisting of counterpoints.

The vaulting of the north aisle is decorated with paintings depicting the life of Thomas Aquinas. In one of the scenes, he is instructing the Dominicans in the presence of St. Peter and St. Paul; education and the masterful managing of complicated theological and philosophical questions were fundamental for the Dominicans. The last frescoe on the vaulting of the north aisle shows an assembly of monks around a personification of the Church, which is complemented again by St. Thomas Aquinas and also St. Augustine. Under the organ loft, we can see a depiction of the Holy Trinity, while on the organ loft itself there is a reminder of the dark events in the life of the Order: the looting of Agnes monastery in the year 1611, and the murder of Dominican monks by Hussite rebels in front of the Church of St. Kliment.

The main altar is just as intriguing,, featuring a picture from the year 1660 by Antonin Stevens, depicting the establishment of the Dominican Order. The altar is also decorated with statues of St. Gregorius and St. Pius, made in the first half of the eighteenth century by the Baroque sculptor František Ignác Weiss. On the first pillar of the right side aisle, we can admire the altars of St. Barbora and St. John of Nepomuk, after which follows the altar of St. Dominic. The Baroque statues of St. John and Mary Magdalene at the altar of the Seven Sorrows of the Virgin Mary

84

Carving on one of the four Rococo confessionals. In its niches there are angels with symbols of Sin, Redemption, Death, and Salvation.

Close up of the ceiling fresco of St. Dominic and St. Francis preaching to the heretics, to the right scenes from the life of St. Dominic can be seen in the south nave.

were produced by Jan Antonín Quittainer. We can also see the precious Baroque statues of St. Mark and St. John at the altar of St. Catherine of Siena. This masterful carving was done by Ferdinand Maxmilián Brokoff in the year 1720. Figures of St. Francis and St. Augustine from M. Schönherr adorn the last altar of the right aisle, which are dedicated to the Virgin Mary of the Rosary. If we lower our vision toward the floor under the altar, we can see the grave ledger of don Baltazar de Marradas, the Malta knight and Imperial general of Spanish origin who significantly contributed to the victory of the Imperial army in the Battle of White Mountain in the year 1620.

Let's move over now to the left side aisle of the Church of St. Jiljí. If we cross over from the main altar to the end of the left aisle, we come to a halt at the Chapel of St. Vaclav. The statues of St. Joseph and St. John the Baptist from M. Schönherr are accompanied by a depiction of the meeting of St. Vaclav with Radslav Zlický from V. V. Reiner. Next to that, we can see the altar of St. Vincent Ferrari on the wall, created by J. A. Quittainer, along with the Baroque statues of the Evangelists Lucas and Mathias from the first half of the eighteenth century. The next altar is dedicated to St. Florian and St. Laurent. At the first pillar near the central altar, we discover the altar of St. Cross with a crucifix from the fifteenth century, as well as Baroque statues of the Seven Sorrows of the Virgin Mary and St. John by F. I. Weiss. On the next pillar, towards the entrance, there is an altar dedicated to St. Thomas Aquinas, with a central image contributed by Mathias Zimprecht. J. A. Quittainer made his mark here as well, in the form of the multiple statues of angels. The last altar, close to the entrance, is dedicated to St. Dorothy; the creator of the altar painting of the Saint is unknown.

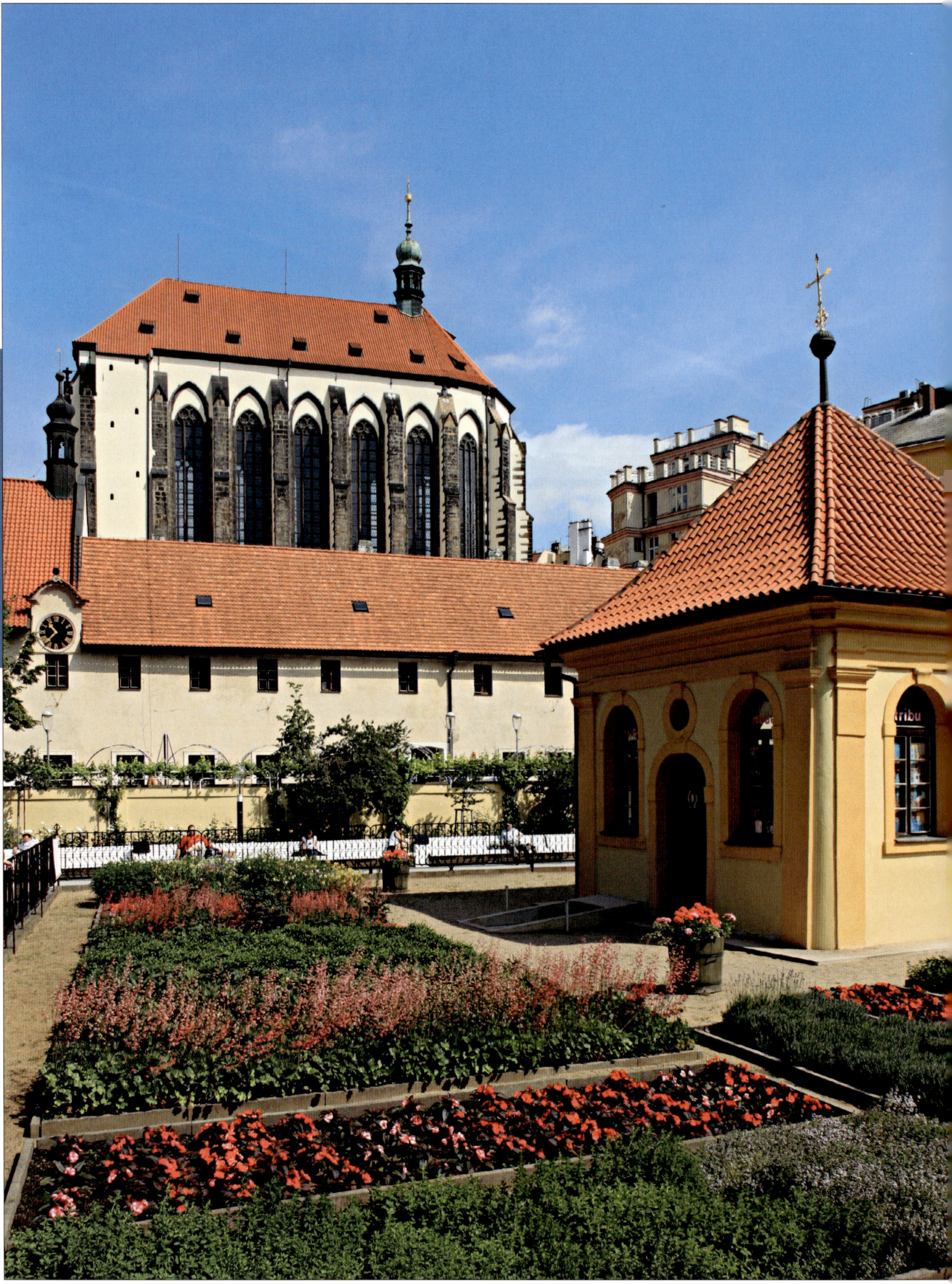

THE CHURCH OF OUR LADY OF THE SNOW, NEW TOWN

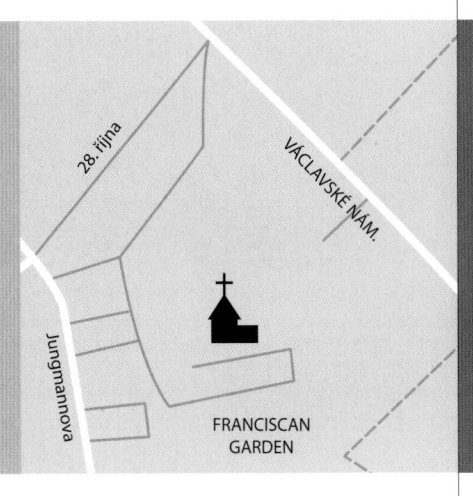

A monumental, originally Gothic three-aisle coronation church, rebuilt in a Baroque style; it was a significant religious and spiritual site in the late medieval Hussite uprising.

Jungmannova Square, Prague 1 – New Town
Transport: Metro A/B Můstek

Worship:
Mon–Fri 7:00 am (apart from summer break), 8:00 am, 6:00 pm, Sat 8:00 am, 6:00 pm, Sun 9:00 am, 11:30 am, 6:00 pm

1347 the church and a Carmelite Monastery were founded
1603 taken over by the Franciscans (minority)
1924–1930 reconstructed

On Jungmann Square, behind an inconspicuous portal, hidden behind the largest three-aisle church in Prague's New Town, sits the Church of Our Lady of the Snow. Its establishment is linked with the Order of the Carmelites, who belonged to the begging monastic order until the middle of the thirteenth century. To prevent the Carmelites from depending on alms, the Czech King and Roman Emperor Charles IV gave them an extensive plot of land behind the bulwark of what was then medieval Prague, as well as laying the founding stone of the Church of Our Lady of the Snow on the third of September 1348, a day after his coronation.

The original church project was grandiose, calling for a three-aisle design; the central aisle was designed to reach a length of one hundred meters and the vaulting was supposed to be built to a height of forty meters. However, even though the original plans called for a building which would have outshone even St. Vitus Cathedral in all its splendor, in the end only a presbytery was built, consecrated in the year 1379. At the beginning of the fifteenth century, stonemasons began work on two Gothic towers and the peripheral walls of the aisle; the fate of the rest of the Church, however, was unfortunately closely connected to the tragic events of the late medieval Czech kingdom. At the beginning of the fifteenth

Aerial view of the Church of Our Lady of the Snow and the Franciscan Garden

▶ View of the presbytery, the only part of the monumental temple which was finally realized.

▶ Looting of the Church of Our Lady of the Snow on the 15th of February 1611 on a copperplate engraving by J. Baptista Collaerts

century, some of Jan Hus's followers poured into the church from nearby Bethlehem Chapel, following a passionate dispute with the Carmelites. Under the influence of Wyclif, these new followers urged the reform of the Catholic Church, the non-payment of indulgences for the Pope's war against the Neapoletan King, and a return to the Apostolic Church.

These disputes often escalated into open and violent conflict. In the year 1419, four years after Jan Hus was burned to death, at the Council of Constance, King Václav IV, son of Charles IV and the brother of the much-reviled Emperor Zigmung (who, in the eyes of the Hussites, was directly responsible for Hus's death), finally permitted church service with communion in both methods, administering the body and the blood of the Lord to laypersons. At that time, Jan Želivský, a protector of and unofficial spokesman for the poor, began preaching in the church. On the 30th of June, 1419, the radical wing of the Hussite movement, under the leadership of Želivský, set out to the New Town town hall, where they threw the town councillor, burgomaster, and reeves from the window. The Hussites then murdered twelve men from the town hall directly under their window. This event, which entered Czech history as the first Prague defenestration, carried over into a long-lasting, violent and raging war between the Catholics and the Hussites. During this frenzied war, the church was destroyed a few times; its bell was even shot down from its tower.

During the course of the sixteenth century, the Church of Our Lady of the Snow continued to fall into disrepair, until the point that its vaulting and façade collapsed. The renewal of the church was then assumed by the Order of Barefoot Franciscans, who acquired it in 1603 as a gift from Emperor Rudolph II. The Franciscans replaced the original Gothic vaulting with a netted Renaissance vault, adorned with paintings of the Virgin Mary, the Holy Trinity, and the Saints. In the torso of the Gothic tower, they built an entry portal with a two-storey organ loft. The original presbytery functioned as a church. However, further repairs were made impossible by the Thirty Years' War, and the church remained unfinished. The monastery was then completed under the influence of Baroque architecture, and from the original Gothic building, only the walls of the side aisle remained, whose chapels are dedicated to the Virgin Mary and St. John of Nepomuk.

The interior of the thirty-two-meter tall church space (originally a presbytery) is dominated by one of the most massive altars in architecture: a pillared Baroque altar, which narrows by three degrees to close almost under the top of the vaulting cross with the Crucifixion. The Calvary is complemented by statues of the Virgin Mary and St. John the Evangelist, situated to the side under the cross. The plastic ornamentation of the monumental altar, built in the years 1649–51, originated from the workshop of the carver Arnošt J. Heidelberg. Here we can also see the depiction of the legend that gave the church its name. According to the story, a wealthy Roman couple decided to build a church dedicated to the Virgin Mary. Mary herself determined where the church would be built: she had snow fall on a suitable site. Hence the church's name, "The Church of Our Lady of the Snow". We also shouldn't overlook a Baroque painting by Reiner, "The Annunciation", situated on the left side aisle, or the mosaic of the Virgin Mary, created by Viktor Foerster, which decorates the Renaissance entry portal.

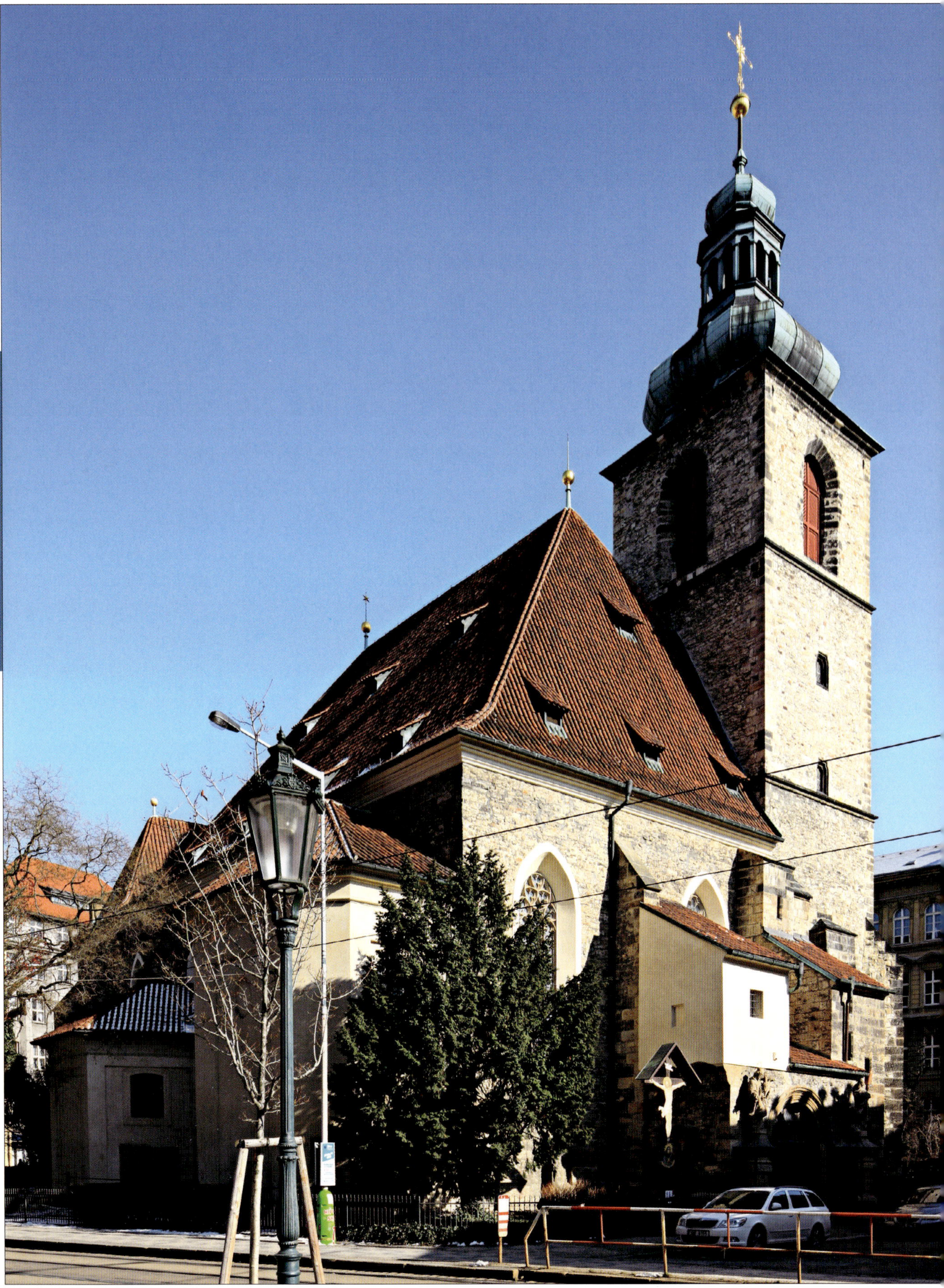

THE CHURCH OF ST. HENRY AND KUNHUTA

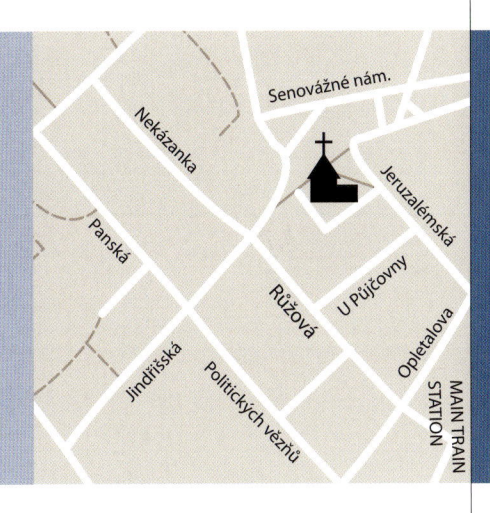

One of the oldest Gothic churchs in the New Town section of Prague, with a monumental Gothic bell tower and rich Baroque ornamentation

Jindřišská st., Prague 1 - New Town
Transport Tram 3, 9, 14, 24 Jindřišská
Worship:
Tue 6:30 am (on Advent), 6:30 pm (besides Advent), Wed 6:00 pm (Slovak), Thu 4:00 pm, Fri 6:00 pm (Slovak), Sun 9:30 am, 10:30 am (Slovak)

1350 founded and consecrated
15th century - Utraquist
1622 Catholic again
17th century - Baroque modifications
End of the 19th century - Regothization

On bustling Jindřišská Street, most busy pedestrians merely catch a glimpse of the massive, Gothic belfry built from blackened stone blocks. The church, separated from the belfry by a tram lane, usually goes unnoticed. But these hurrying visitors have just passed by one of the oldest churches in the New Town section of Prague, whose construction was directly connected to the construction of New Town itself. That magnanimous, urbanistic plan, unparalleled in contemporary medieval Europe, was approved by Charles IV in the year 1347 at Křivoklát Castle.

The sanctuary, dedicated to St. Jindřich (Henry) and his wife St. Kunhuta, was built in the Luxembourg Gothic style in 1350 as a three-aisle, non-basilica church. It became the main parish church of the lower part of New Town, while the Church of St. Steven, of a similar design, was the parish church in the upper part. The massive belfry, originally made of wood, was added between 1472 and 1476, receiving its current Renaissance appearance in the 1670s. At the end of the nineteenth century it underwent a Gothic renovation, and today is known to Prague dwellers as Jindřich's Tower.

The church rode out the Hussite wars without damage, and from the very beginning the Eucharist was actually celebrated in it with the communion under both methods.

Looking towards the tower of St Jindřich which juts out on the left behind the temple tower on the left.

View of the main nave towards the altar

▶ View of the presbytery. The church is decorated with plenty of late-Baroque paintings, in front a Rococo wooden pulpit is visible.

in 1648, a few years after the Thirty Years' War, Swedish soldiers were dug in in front of the New Town fortification wall. Although Prague citizens defended the city from the New Town bulwark, one of the targets which the Swedes managed to shoot was St. Jindřich Church and particularly its belfry. The damaged church required expensive repairs from its war days, which provided the church with new Baroque features.

After the Thirty Years' War, the Baroque alterations continued and the church acquired another two chapels: the Chapel of Our Lady of the Visitation was built first, in the year 1685, with the Chapel of St. Lucas following about eleven years later. However, it was soon evident that the additions of the chapels were far from adequate and that the church needed more extensive repairs. The interior of the church therefore underwent further Baroque-style modifications from 1738 to 1741. All of that work could have easily gone to waste, though, because in the summer of 1745 the roof caught fire from a lightning strike. The roof burned down and the roof frame collapsed; the subsequent repairs to the roof lasted until 1752. Further misfortune came in the form of the road placed between the belfry and the church, which is a tram track today.

Right at the entrance to the church, we can first stop at the statue of St. John of Nepomuk, probably created by Michal Brokoff, and on the other side of the entry portal at the statue of St. Jude, whose creator is unknown. Now we'll go through the Renaissance vestibule and arrive in the church aisle. On the vault of the organ loft, we can see the sculpted bosom of Queen Kunhuta; at the end of the church space is the Baroque altar, complemented by a painting from the year 1698. The painting, made by J. J. Heinsch, depicts two scenes: in the first, St. Jindřich is protecting Prague from Swedish soldiers, while in the second scene his wife St. Kunhuta is crossing over a white-hot plow blade, in order to provide proof of her faithfulness to her husband. Jindřich, canonized in the year 1146, was first the Bavarian Duke, then the Roman King, and finally, in 1014, became the Emperor of the Holy Roman Empire. Themes from the lives of St. Jindřich and St. Kunhuta can also be seen in paintings located in the presbytery painted in the first half of the eighteenth century by Siardus Nosecký, a member of the Premonstratensian Order.

But now back to the altar! Along its side we can admire the Baroque statues of St. Wenceslas and St. Vojtěch which were created by J. J. Bendl in 1650. If we shift over to the façade of the left side aisle, we come to the altar of the Holy Trinity with a painting from Karel Škréta Jr., from the year 1685. There's another valuable paintingin the Chapel of St. Barbora, which is next to the left aisle. The painting of St. Barbora on the first altar of the chapel was created by the Bavarian painter Mathias Zimprecht in 1673. The other altar of the chapel is dedicated to the Virgin Mary and accompanied by Baroque statues of St. Rocha, St. Sebastian, St. Wenceslas, and St. John of Nepomuk; their creators are not known.

From the Chapel of St. Barbora, we come next to the Chapel of St. Lucas, featuring a Baroque painting of St. Lucas and St. Joseph by J. J. Heinsch. In the left side aisle we can see an altar in the façade dedicated to Our Lady of the Visitation, with a painting by Škréta on this subject. There is also a chapel connected to the right aisle, likewise dedicated to Our Lady of the Visitation and featuring paintings from V. V. Reiner. For spiritual refreshment we can also visit Jindřich's Tower, where there is now an exhibition about the history of Prague towers and belfries. The intellectual experience can be enhanced by a pleasant spell of musing over a coffee in the restaurant located in the St. Jindřich bell tower.

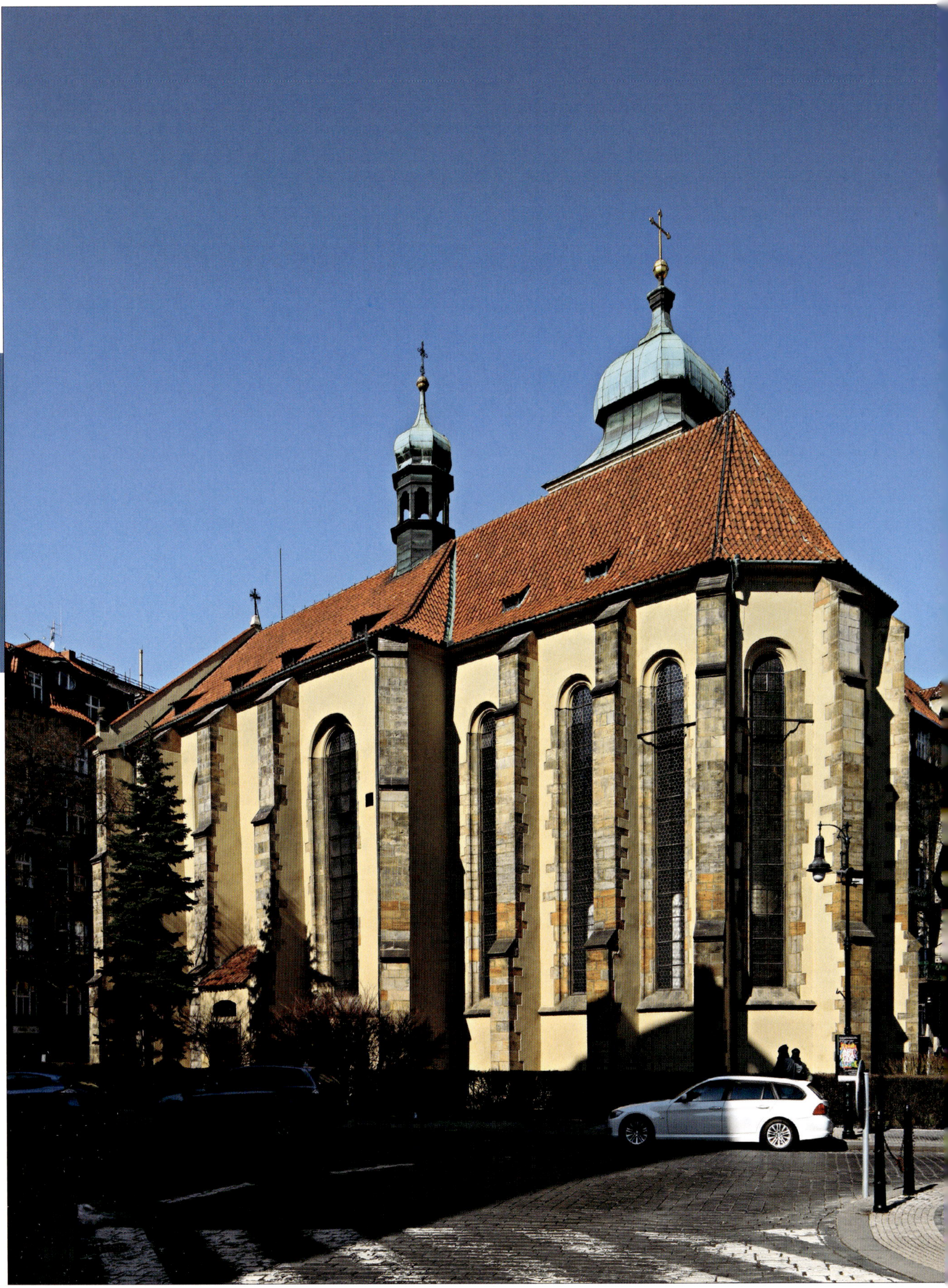

THE CHURCH OF THE HOLY GHOST

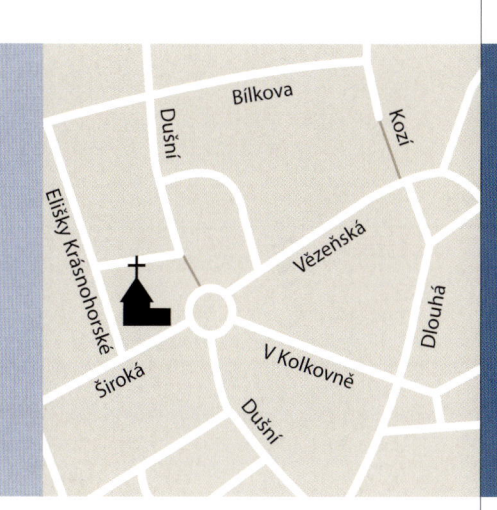

A Gothic church standing in the midst of neo-Gothic and neo-Classical town buildings in the Old Town section of Prague, the former border of the Jewish ghetto.

U Sv. Ducha st. Prague 1 - Old Town

Transport Metro A Staroměstská, Tram 17, 18 Staroměstská

Church service: Sun 9:30 am

1348 a Benedictine monastery was built and consecrated
1420 closure of the monastery, Utraquists (German language)
17th century Baroque reconstruction

The small space which the Gothic Church of the Holy Ghost occupies today, in the neighbourhood of the Spanish Synagogue, was almost empty up until the middle of the fourteenth century, merely containing some small townhomes. Things changed in the 1440s, when wealthy Prague townsman Mikuláš Rokycanský dedicated a significant sum to the establishment of a Benedictine monastery. The original construction was demolished, and the establishment of a monastery with a small church was confirmed in 1348 by the archbishop Arnošt of Pardubice.

Construction took place very quickly and the first Benedictine nuns relocated here from the monastery of St. George at the Castle. Their Order soon begin to expand, mostly among the daughters of rich Prague townsmen. However, the calm lifestyle of the Benedictines was soon disturbed by the Hussite uprising. The nuns were forced out in 1420, the property of the monastery was partly stolen and partly sold, and the church began to be used by the Prague German Ultraquists. A couple of decades later the monastery was hit by another catastrophe: during a storm, lightning set fire to the monastery roof. The roof frame burned down and the façade gable was split open by the heat and collapsed to the earth, burying many people in its rubble.

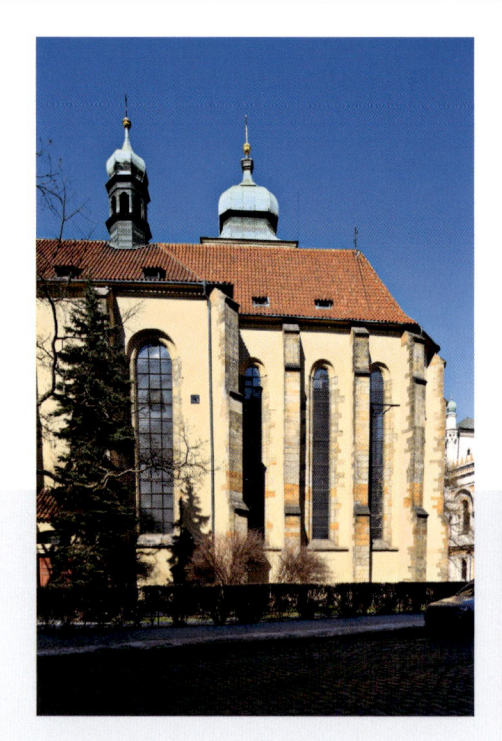

Very close to the church of the Holy Ghost is the Spanish Synagogue (see pp. 128–131), whose Moorish curves are visible on the right behind the apse.

View of the main nave

▶ Late Baroque altar from around 1740. The main altarpiece features a modern (around 1890) picture of the Descent of the Holy Spirit, in the extension there is an image of the Holy Trinity.

Under the reign Emperor Rudolph II and his supporters of secret magical and alchemy disciplines, the decaying church and monastery were luckily acquired by the Benedictines from St. George at the Castle. This was done with the caveat that the maintenance of the local spiritual administrator would be on the account of the St. George Benedictines. In order fulfill the Emperor's conditions, the nuns had a separate vicarage built here. However, fickle fate continued to persecute the church and on the 21st of June in 1689 it was engulfed in another massive blaze, which likewise destroyed significant sections of both Old Town and New Town. It was soon established that the fire had been set by agents of the French King.

For the Church of the Holy Ghost, the fire represented a catastrophe: the sanctuary completely burned down to its foundation, its vault collapsed, and only the charred, peripheral walls with their supportive pillars showed that a relatively large Gothic church had once been here. The subsequent reconstruction lasted three years and the church acquired a new Baroque vault. Unlike a whole range of other Prague churches, the Church of the Holy Grail wasn't affected by Joseph's reforms, and it has thus retained its form to the present day. The insensitive redevelopment of Old Town and the Jewish ghetto, which began in the year 1890 and spoiled many valuable Middle Age constructions, removed many small town buildings as well as farm buildings from the church's immediate vicinity. Then, in the year 1932, the vicarage standing at the church was also demolished.

As has already been mentioned, the church was situated in close proximity to the Jewish Ghetto, now the Jewish Quarter. For the Jewish inhabitants, their closeness to the Church of the Holy Ghost meant that they were obliged to attend Catholic sermons here and, up until 1785, pay the local bell-ringer a special tax, called *Glöckelgeld*; the ringing was intended to warn against the storms and floods which tormented Old Town with dismal regularity.

The inner furnishings of the church are only partially original, with a whole series of objects having been brought from other churches and religious buildings; the most ob-

97

Francis Xavier preaches unto the Gentiles, relief on the gate of the altar

Gothic Pieta from around 1400, the author probably came from the circle of the Master of the Týn Crucifixion.

vious example is a massive, late Baroque portal-type altar, brought over from the Church of St. Cross the Greater. The St. Cross church was built close to the Vltava, not far from the Church of the Holy Ghost, probably on the site of today's Hotel Intercontinental. That church, founded by Přemysl Otakar II in 1256 in commemoration of the victory over Prussian soldiers and entrusted to the care of the Cyriaks, didn't survive the Enlightenment reforms, and Emperor Joseph II eventually shut it down in 1783. The abandoned church fell into disrepair, and it was demolished at the beginning of the Old Prague rehabilitation in 1890. The side altar of the St. Cross church was rescued and later became the main altar at The Church of the Holy Ghost. The painting *The Sending of the Holy Ghost*, which forms its mid-point, is much more recent, however, and originated symbolically from 1890, when the hasty and, from today's architectural and art historical perspective, unforgivable Prague rehabilitation began.

Other parts of the altar are from an earlier date, however. The smaller Baroque painting in the altar extension, depicting the Holy Trinity, dates back to the middle of the eighteenth century, while the two gates along the side of the altar body can be traced back to the year 1730. They aren't original either, having originated from the Church of St. Bartholomew, which also fell victim to Joseph's reforms. On the doors of these gates, we can admire a relief depicting St. Francis Xavier, preaching to the pagans and baptizing the Black King. The statues on the gate date back to the first half of the eighteenth century and were taken over from the Church of St. Cross the Greater. The wooden draperies, featuring an image of St. Joseph from J. J. Heinsch, and a pontifical chair located in the presbytery both originate from the Church of St. Simon and St. Jude. In the presbytery there is also an early Baroque statue of St. Sebastian, probably from the master J. J. Bendl; this is followed by the altar of John of Nepomuk, and on the opposite side an opulent, relief-decorated pulpit with scenes of the sickness and death of St. Francis Xavier. These artifacts were also transferred to the Church of the Holy Ghost from the Church of St. Bartholomew.

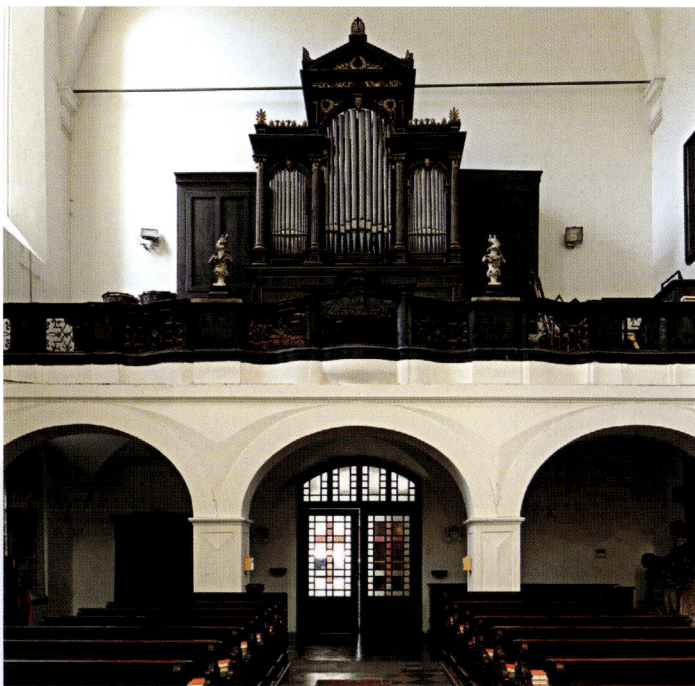

Pulpit

Organ from the 19th century

In the church aisle itself, We can see another four altars in the church aisle itself. Near the north side of the church we can see the altar of St. Otylia and St. Jude Thaddeus, with a painting of St. Vojtěch and side statues of St. Onufrius, St. Dismas, and the penitent rogue at Jesus's right side. On the south side, we mustn't overlook the altar of the Holiest Heart of the Virgin Mary, adorned by Baroque paintings from the middle of the eighteenth century and also the altar of St. Laurent. In the north side of the church, there are non-traditional sculptures in the altar from the beginning of the eighteenth century, which are actually figures depicting both a sitting Christ and Christ with bound hands. We also should take notice of three hanging paintings from the cusp of the eighteenth century, depicting St. Vaclav with Emperor Henry, victorious Czechs under St. Wenceslas's banner, and, lastly, the Final Judgement.

However, the oldest and most artistically valuable artifact can be found in the space under the church organ loft: a stone, bigger-than-life-size Pieta sculpture, dating back to the year 1400. This artifact, a late-Gothic sculptural production, has a similarly troubling fate as the whole Church of the Holy Ghost. The Pieta was also originally built in the Church of St. Cross the Greater; however, during the Hussite frenzy, its head was knocked off. The head was found in the year 1627, and so it was possible to restore the Pieta, and at the end of the nineteenth century, it was transferred to the Church of the Holy Ghost. Today, there is also a statue of St. John of Nepomuk in front of it, giving alms. This statue, like many of the artistic artifacts in the Church of the Holy Ghost, was originally somewhere else, actually near to today's Hotel International.

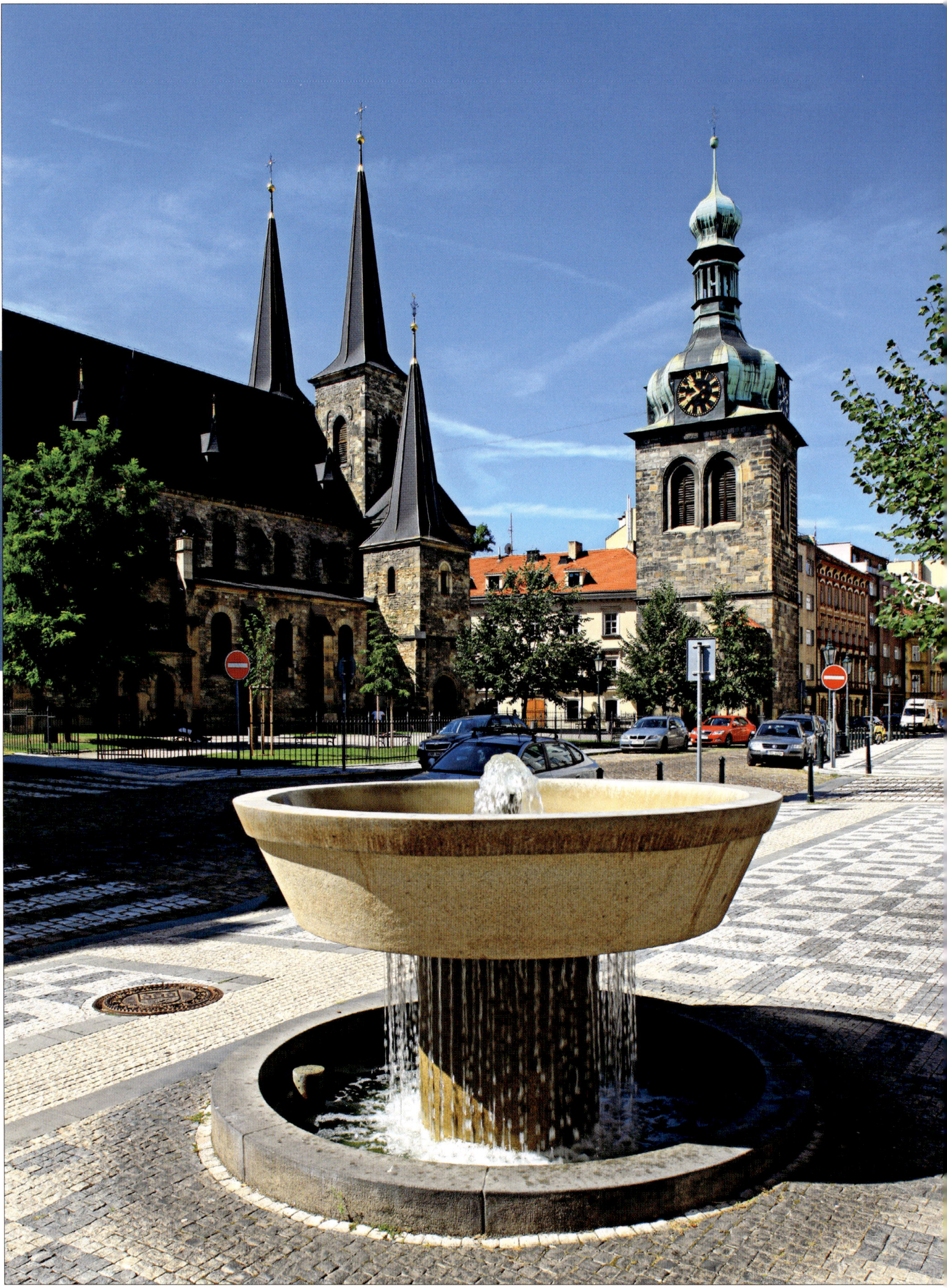

THE CHURCH OF ST. PETER

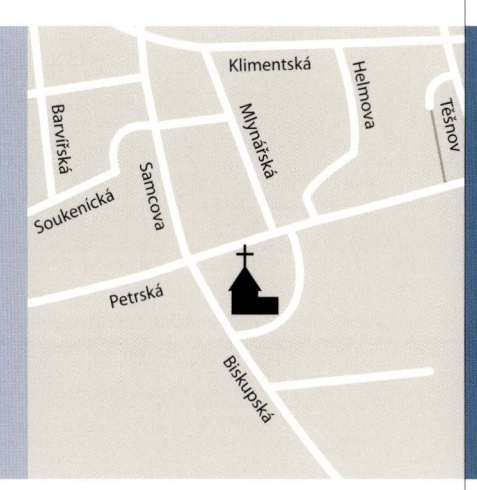

A huge Gothic church with a Gothic bell tower

Biskupská st., Prague 1 - New Town
Transport: Metro B, C Florenc, Tram
Worship:
Sun 10:30 am, Wed, Fri 4:30 pm
Around the year 1080 The Church of St. Peter with the Plebans
1215 commandery of the Teutonic Knights
1413 parish administered by Crusader priests

If we go from the Old Town and cross over Revoluční Street, where there was originally a medieval bulwark, we come to Peter's Quarter, which is a part of New Town and is shut off from the north of the Vltava. Beyond Peter's Quarter, back in the middle of the nineteenth century, Prague ended and the village, which dragged from there along the bank of the Vltava to the northeast, was still awaiting its connection to the hundred-spired city. Peter's Quarter acquired its name according to the Gothic church, which looks black against the sky on the small square and is a short distance behind the renowned White Swan department store.

Originally at this site, referred to as Na Poříčí, there was a settlement of German merchants. Around the middle of the twelfth century, a large three-aisle basilica with a Romanesque style apse was built. The Germans left the often-flooded area at the beginning of the thirteenth century, and the basilica was donated to the Order of German Knights. When the basilica found itself outside the protected zone after the bulwark around Old Town was completed in 1230, the Germans came to the conclusion that it would be better to find a safer base inside the fortification system. This happened in the year 1235, and the Knights built the Church of St. Benedict where another legendary

Close up of a Baroque pulpit with reliefs of the snake in the desert, the Finding of the Holy Cross and the Exaltation of the Holy Cross and with statues of the four Fathers of the Church

▶ The main altar of St. Peter with a painting depicting Christ handing the keys to St Peter.

deparment store, Kotva, stands today. The orphaned St. Peter's basilica was given as a gift by Queen Constance to the Knights of the Cross with the Red Star; however, even they didn't last longer than seventeen years, so after 1252 the Church of St. Peter ceased to function as a religious order sanctuary and became a parish church for the local settlement.

About a hundred years later, the decaying Romanesque basilica was rebuilt. In approximately 1382 its northern aisle was demolished and replaced by two much larger Gothic aisles. Another thirty years later, the south aisle and apse were torn down; the newly modified central aisle with the Gothic presbytery, the north aisle, and the south Romanesque aisle remained. In this somewhat stylistically and architecturally disorganized state, the Church of St. Peter, now mostly rebuilt in a Gothic style, came face-to-face with the Hussite uprising.

Regarding the observation of the Eucharist, the original compromise (that both methods would be observed alternately) was soon proven unsuccessful. At the main altar in the central aisle, the Eucharist was observed by administering under both methods, while at the side altar only the body of Christ was given. Among young altar boys, the initial light bantering grew into mutual, hateful attacks. During a parish fair in 1419, a dispute between altar boys turned into a free-for-all, in which other church service members also joined in. The incident resulted in one death and the expulsion of a Catholic priest. However, the unpleasant matter had a positive effect on the church in the end, for it stayed exclusively Ultraquist, which protected it from looting and burning in the subsequent Hussite Wars.

The somewhat awkward, stylistically impure design of The Church of St. Peter forced the demolition of the original Romanesque aisle at the end of the fifteenth century, which was replaced by a wide side aisle in late Gothic style. The church thereby acquired a completely new vault. In the year 1628, the Church of St. Peter returned to Catholic hands, specifically to the Knights of the Cross with the Red Star. However, the first church services only took place four years later. The seventeenth century wasn't a

103

Crucifix to the left of the main entrance

Evening view of St. Peter and Peter's tower

calm period for the church of St. Peter. When the Swedes sieged Prague after the Thirty Years' War, the church was significantly damaged during the bombardment. A second blow was struck by a fire, which broke out in October of 1680 at a nearby mill; the rectory burned down and the roof and roof frame of the church were destroyed. Fortunately, the vault fortunately survived the intense heat. But, only nine years later, flames once again engulfed Prague rooftops, and this time the fire damaged the Church of St. Peter much more considerably. Archbishop Jan Bedřich of Valdštejn, the Grandmaster of the Order of the Cross – similarly as in the first fire – once again took the reconstruction of the church into his own hands. During the Prussian siege of Prague in the year 1757, the church also suffered a few blows from Prussian cannons. The Church of St. Peter, which had acquired some Baroque elements from its reconstruction after the fires, continued to fall into disrepair, and in the second part of the nineteenth century it was than obvious that a complete reconstruction was necessary.

Reconstruction began in 1878 and, under the growing influence of neo-Romanticism, its determining features were an attempt at a Gothic renovation. The delicate reconstruction, which was led by Joseph Mocker, was mostly limited to the removal of the Baroque ornaments, the Baroque stucco plastering, and the alteration of some windows in order to revive their original Gothic appearance. The main portal also underwent a Gothic renovation, newly adorned with figures of Christ and St. Peter by the sculptor Ludvík Šimek. The Gothic form of the Church of St. Peter was thereby restored to a great extent, although the south wall of the central aisle, with its two arcade pillars, bears traces of the original Romanesque design.

The furniture in St. Peter's dates back to the Baroque period. First of all, we shouldn't overlook the central altar from the year 1740, decorated with statues of St. Paul and St. John the Baptist. The altar is complemented by a relief depicting the liberation of Peter from prison and the beheading of St. Peter. We then come to an altar painting made by V. V. Reiner in 1730, featuring a motif of Christ

Baroque statue of St. John of Nepomuk from the mid-18th century on the south wall of the presbytery

handing over a key to St. Peter. The south wall of the presbytery is adorned with a statue of John of Nepomuk and a crucifix; both works are from the middle of the eighteenth century. The last part of the south aisle is decorated by the altar of The Virgin Mary of the Assumption, from the first half of the eighteenth century. In the south aisle we can also take delight in a Baroque statue of St. Peter.

The end of the north aisle is capped by the altar of Mary Magdalene, with an altar painting depicting Mary Magdalene rejecting jewels and the vanity of the mundane world. At the pillars between the aisles, we can stop at the altar of St. Barbora from the middle of the eighteenth century with a painting entitled *St. Barbora with the Angels*. The picture in the extension of this altar depicts the death of St. Barbora, complemented by statues of St. Wenceslas and St. George. At the next pillar we can pause at the Baroque altar of St. Florian, which is dominated by a painting of St. Florian made by the master Petr Molitor in the middle of the eighteenth century. The pulpit also dates back to the same period. It has a relief of the Four Fathers of the Church and motifs of the Discovery of St. Cross, The Promotion of St. Cross and the Serpent in the Desert.

From an architectural as well as a historical perspective, it is very interesting that the Church of St. Peter was surrounded by a cemetery in past centuries. Perhaps its very proximity gave rise to the legend of a local gravedigger. The gravedigger was good way down deep in his heart, but he happily indulged in some of the Devil's pleasures, especially card gambling. In the evenings he would meet up with his two companions, a parish clerk and a barrel maker. They used to sit in a pub called Avens and play cards. However, one day the dreaded Black Death entered the city. The plague marched inexorably though the winding little streets of Prague, lurking in the damp courtyards and dark corners and haunting the sagging rooftops of Old Town. People were dying in droves and the gravedigger had a lot of work and therefore a lot of money. So he sat with his friends in the evenings at Avens even more frequently and played cards into the wee hours of the morning. However, one day it happened that he sat down for beer and cards

106

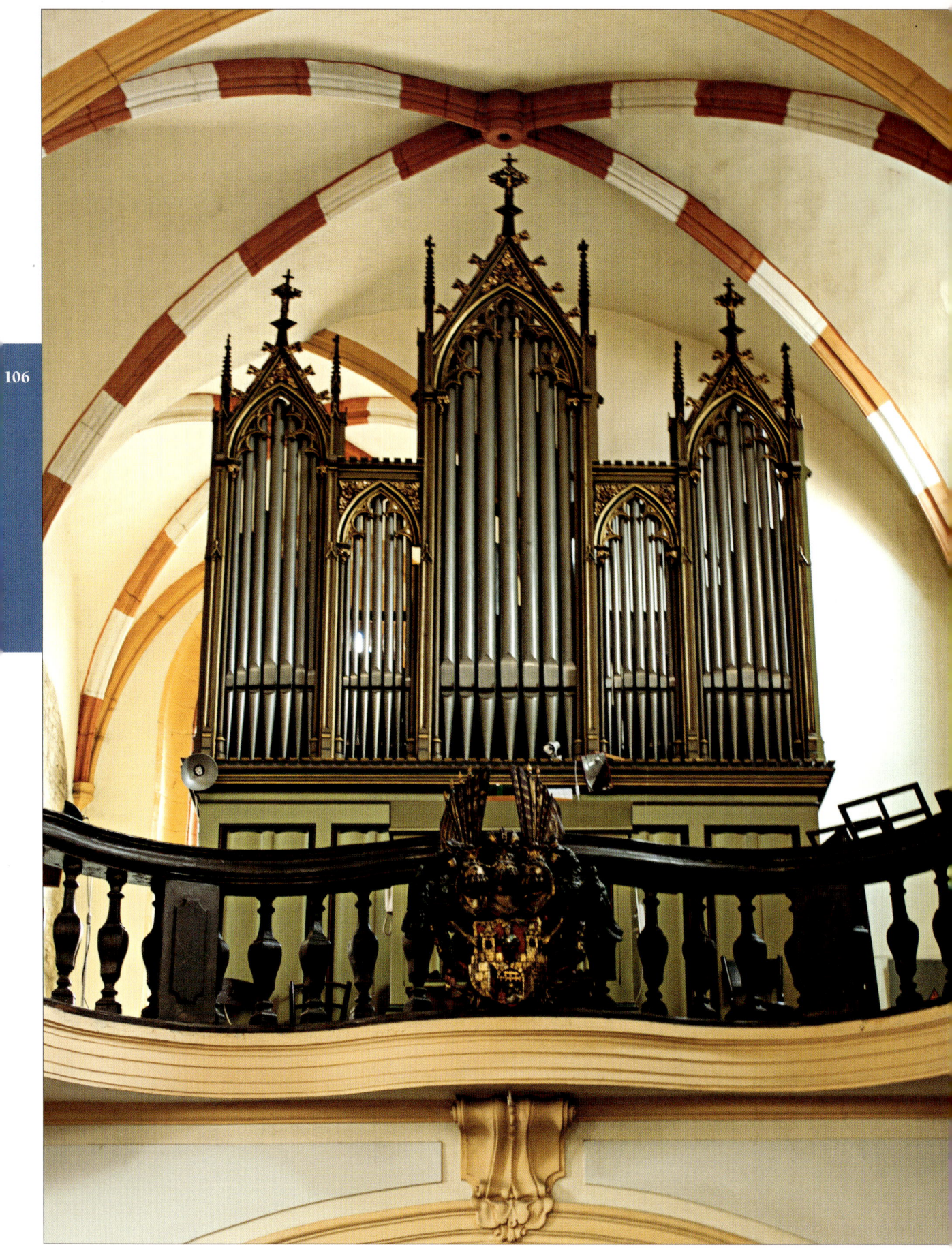

Close up of the main altar from the year 1740

◀ Organ

at Avens alone, his friends having finally succumbed to the Black Death. The gravedigger was shattered. In the ink-black dark of night, he finally set off to St. Peter's morgue. He knelt down in front of the cold, motionless bodies of his friends and imploringly called them to one last round of cards. Suddenly, the dead men's bodies moved; their contorted limbs straightened; their eyes shone wildly in their collapsed holes. Their bodies sat up on the slab, and the revived corpses began to shuffle through the cards. The gravedigger played cards with his dead friends as if he was playing for his own life. However, around midnight it started to thunder and a strong, unexpected gust of wind forced open the small window and blew out the flickering flame of the candle. A long, terrible silence descended on the morgue. In the morning, the parishioners found three bodies in the open morgue, their yellowed fingers clenching their last dealt cards. The barrel maker and the parish clerk were each given a Christian burial, but the gravedigger found no peace. And that's why on stormy nights, he goes around the Church of St. Peter pleading with night-time visitors to play a game of cards with him. Only the brave player who fleeces him can free the gravedigger and return peace to his soul.

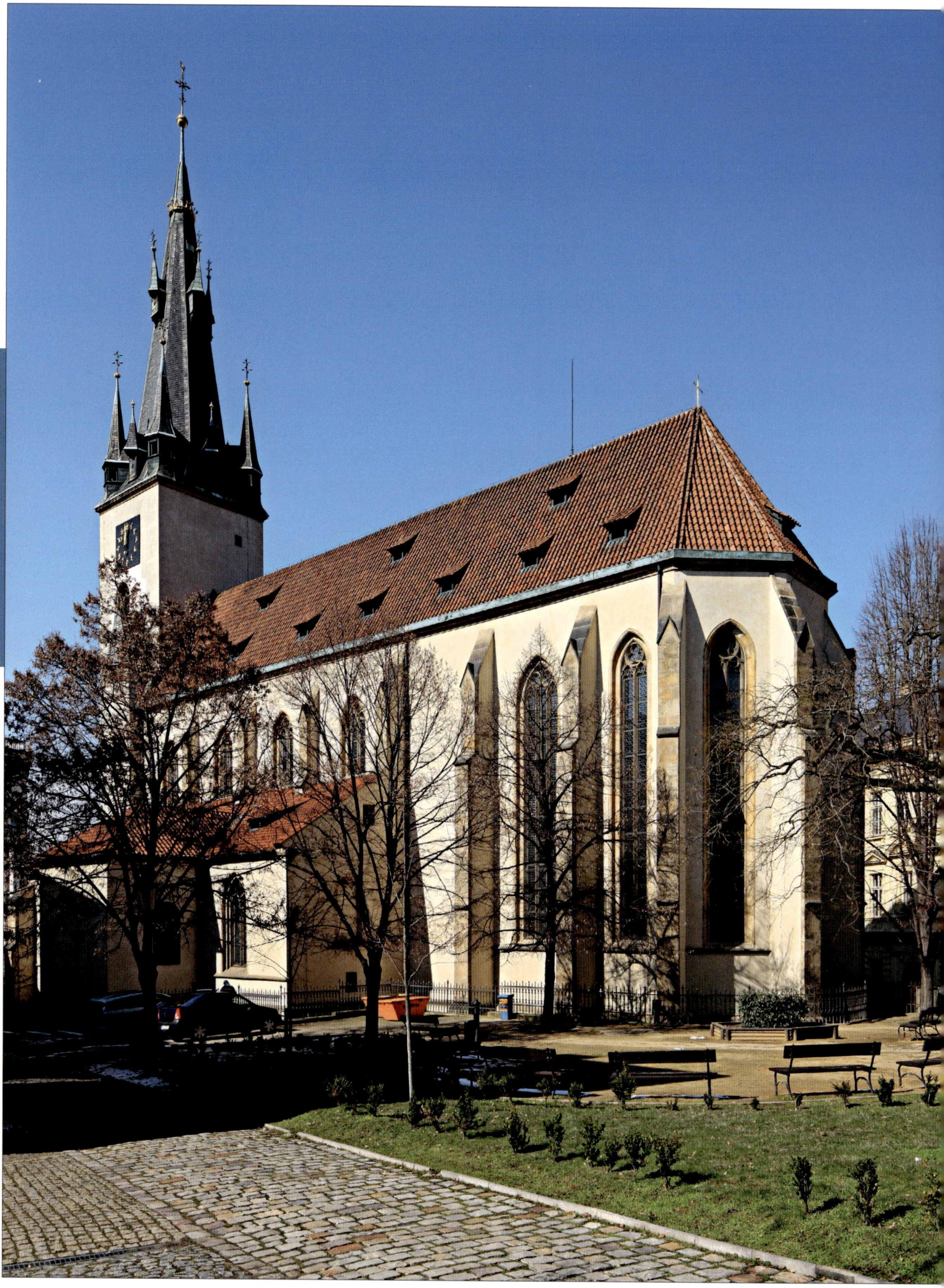

THE CHURCH OF ST. STEVEN

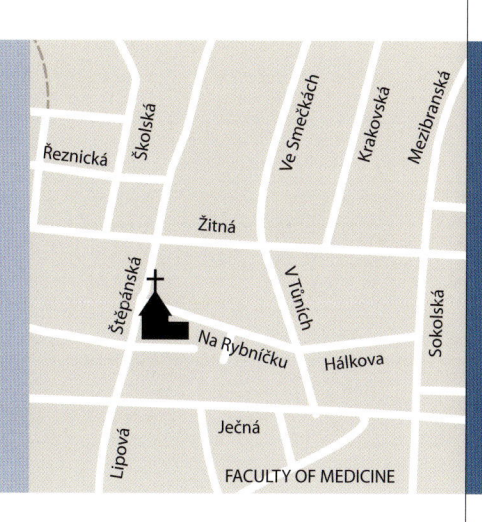

A Gothic, three-aisle basilica from the late Middle Ages, with opulently decorated furnishings

Ječná 505/2, Prague 2 - New Town
Transport: Metro A, B Můstek, B, C Muzeum, Tram 4, 10, 16, 22 Štěpánská
Worship:
Sun 11:00 am

1352 parish established
1392 construction completed
1419 Sub utraque species
1621 Catholic again

The Church of St. Steven was founded as a parish church for the upper part of New Town by Charles IV. Its construction began in the year 1351 and it was completed in the year 1392. St. Steven's acquired the shape of a three aisle-basilica. In the year 1401, a four-sided tower with four miniature turrets in the corners was built into the middle of the façade. The choice of St Steven as the church's patron saint is somewhat unusual; there are not too many churches in the Czech Republic dedicated to this saint. St. Steven was evidently one of the first Christian martyrs. The Jewish order accused him of blasphemy at the age of 35, and as a result Steven was stoned to death.

Over the centuries, the building underwent various modifications and additions. At the end of the seventeenth century a chapel was added on to the south aisle with the tomb of the Kornel family. Here we can find the early Baroque altar of the Descent of the Cross, complemented by statues of St. Gregorius and St. John the Baptist, probably from the workshop of J. J. Bendl. We should also carefully note the precious painting of Christ under the cross from the year 1680. The remains of precious Gothic murals were uncovered in this chapel as recently as the 1990s.

The early Baroque black-and-gold central portal altar dates back to the year 1669 and is decorated by a large

Gothic stone pulpit (circa 1500)

The altarpiece the Stoning of St. Stephen from the 17th century by M. Zimprecht

▶ View of the main nave in the direction of the altar

polychromic statues of St. Wenceslas and St. Ludmila, while in the upper part of the altar we can see the Virgin Mary, St. John the Evangelist and Mary Magdalene. The sculptural ornamentation probably came from the workshop of J. J. Bendl. The altar is complemented by two paintings: a main painting and an extension. The first painting depicts the stoning of St. Steven, while the subject of the second painting is the Holy Trinity. Both pictures were created in the year 1672 by Mathias Zimprecht, who was a follower of Karel Škréta.

If we cross over to the south, or right, aisle, the altar of the Seven Sorrows of the Virgin Mary grabs our attention, decorated by an early Baroque Pieta from the year 1638. At the first pillar of the south aisle we can also delight in the altar of St. Rosalie from the year 1745. The north, or left, aisle is dominated by the altar of the Baptism of Christ, a late Baroque work from the year 1720; then, at the pillar we find an altar dedicated to St. Ann with a painting of the saint from J. Scheiwl from the year 1880. The next altar of the Virgin Mary St. Steven with a Gothic painting of the Holy Mother is also noteworthy. The painting most likely comes from the fifteenth century. The church ornamentation is complemented by a series of preserved gravestones from the sixteenth and seventeenth centuries. We should also add that one of the greatest masters of Baroque sculpture, Matyáš Bernard Braun, was also buried here in 1738. If we go outside, we'll also notice a late Gothic bell tower, built from 1600–1605 on the location of the former cemetery, whose existence is commemorated by two stone crosses.

In the year 1419, both methods of communion were observed at St. Steven's church, which clearly saved the church from total devastation in the ensuing Hussite Wars. The Ultraquists remained in the Church of St. Steven until the year 1621.

111

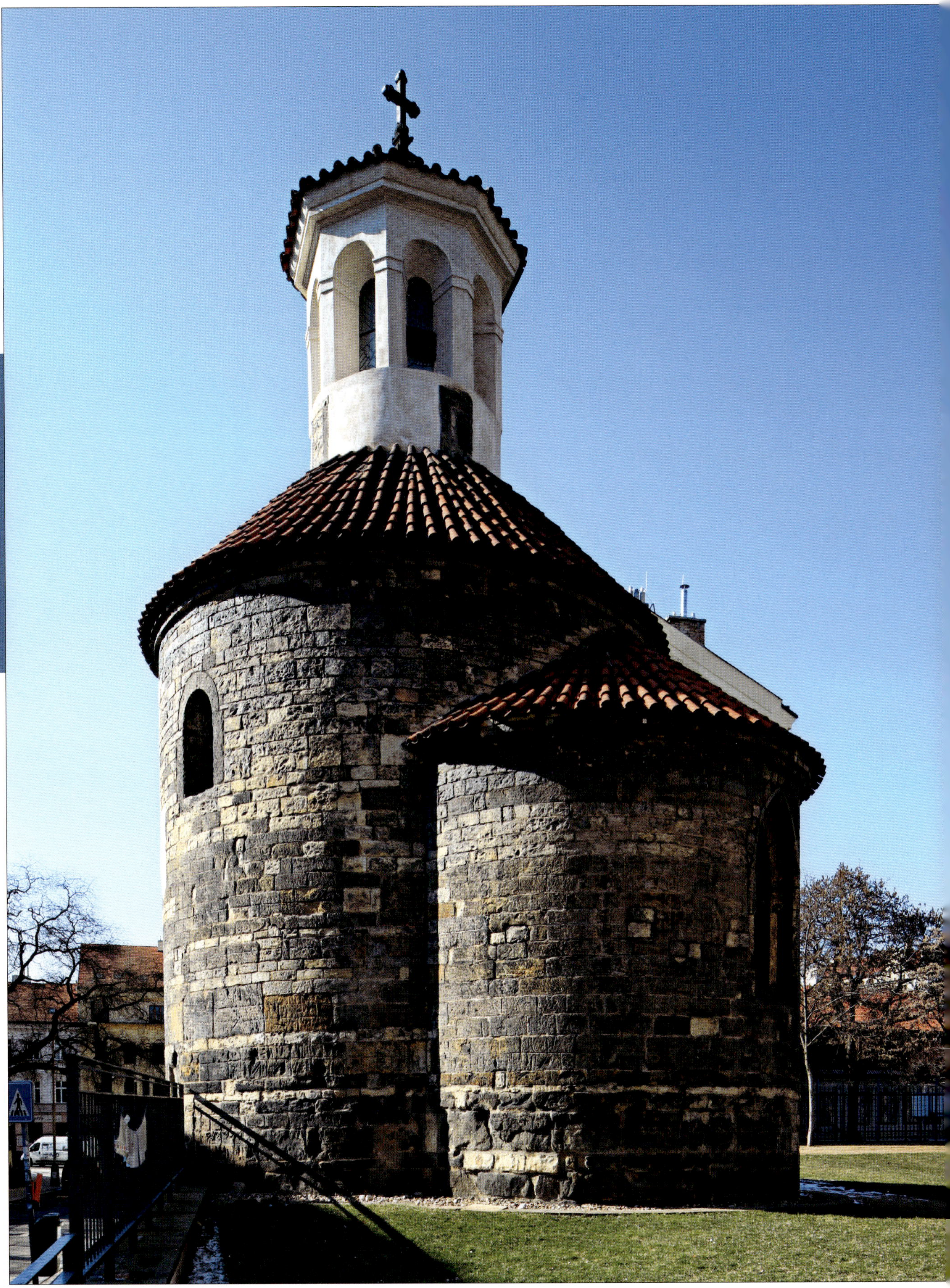

ST. LONGIN'S ROTUNDA

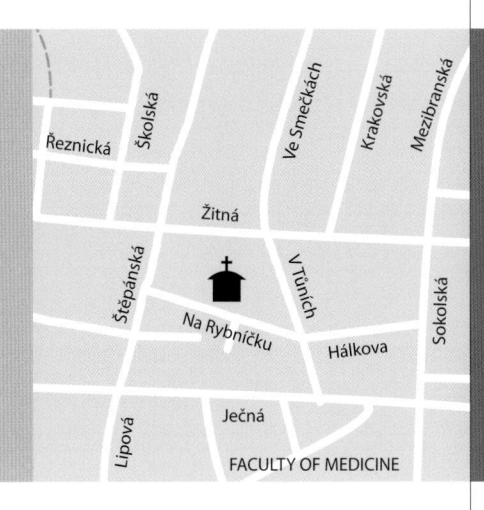

The second-oldest Romanesque rotunda in Prague, poetically located in the shadow of the Gothic Church of St. Steven

Na Rybníčku, Prague 2 - New Town
Transport: Metro A, B Můstek, B, C Muzeum, Tram 4, 10, 16, 22 Štěpánská

Built at the beginning of the 12th century as a parish
14th century - dedicated to St. Longin
17th century - Baroque reconstruction and extension of the lanterns
1783 desecrated

Back in the tenth century, a tiny, ancient settlement called Rybníček (Little Pond) is mentioned in the annals, located near where Štěpánská Street is today, listed as property of Břevnov Monastery in the year 993. In this place rich with water springs, there was originally a pagan sanctuary; after the acceptance of Christianity in the Czech principality, the smallest (and currently the second oldest) Romanesque rotunda in Prague was built on the same site. It was complemented by a cemetery, in which foreigners were buried in the time of the Plague. The rotunda was dedicated to St. Steven up until the fourteenth century, to whom the parish standing next to it was also dedicated in 1351, founded by King Charles IV. The new Gothic Church of St. Steven then became the spiritual center and main church for the upper part of the New Town area of Prague.

The rotunda was, in all likelihood - in light of its inclusion in the property of the Břevnov monastery - built by the Benedictines, in the first third of the twelfth century. At the beginning of the thirteenth century it was then transferred over to the holding of the Order of German Knights, who then sold it off to Kunhuta of Hungary, the second wife of Přemysl Otakar II. From her hands, the rotunda wound up as the property of a Lay Hospital Brotherhood, which was founded by Kunhuta's daughter, later known

St. Longin's Rotunda with the Church of St. Steven

as St. Agnes (Anežka, in Czech). After the building of the Church of St. Steven, the rotunda was newly dedicated to St. Longinus, whose remains were brought from Rome by Charles IV. St. Longinus was one of the Roman soldiers who took part in the crucifixion of Christ. It was he who pierced the Saviour's side with his spear. He deeply regretted his deed, and before he was executed, he spent decades repenting and living a hermit's life. Longin's pike, along with the Holy Grail, are the key motifs of Middle Age Arthurian epics.

In the seventeenth century the rotunda acquired a miniature tower, a so-called lantern, illuminating its interior. From the year 1782 it was used as a storage warehouse, and it was only restored to its original purpose in the nineteenth century. Today, we can see a small Baroque altar from the year 1762 in the rotunda. As a matter of interest, we'll add that if we connect St. Longin's rotunda with St. Cross's Lesser rotunda on Karolina Světlá Street, with the bridge tower in Lesser Town, and with St. Vitus Cathedral, we get an azimuth allegedly showing the summer and winter solstices.

115

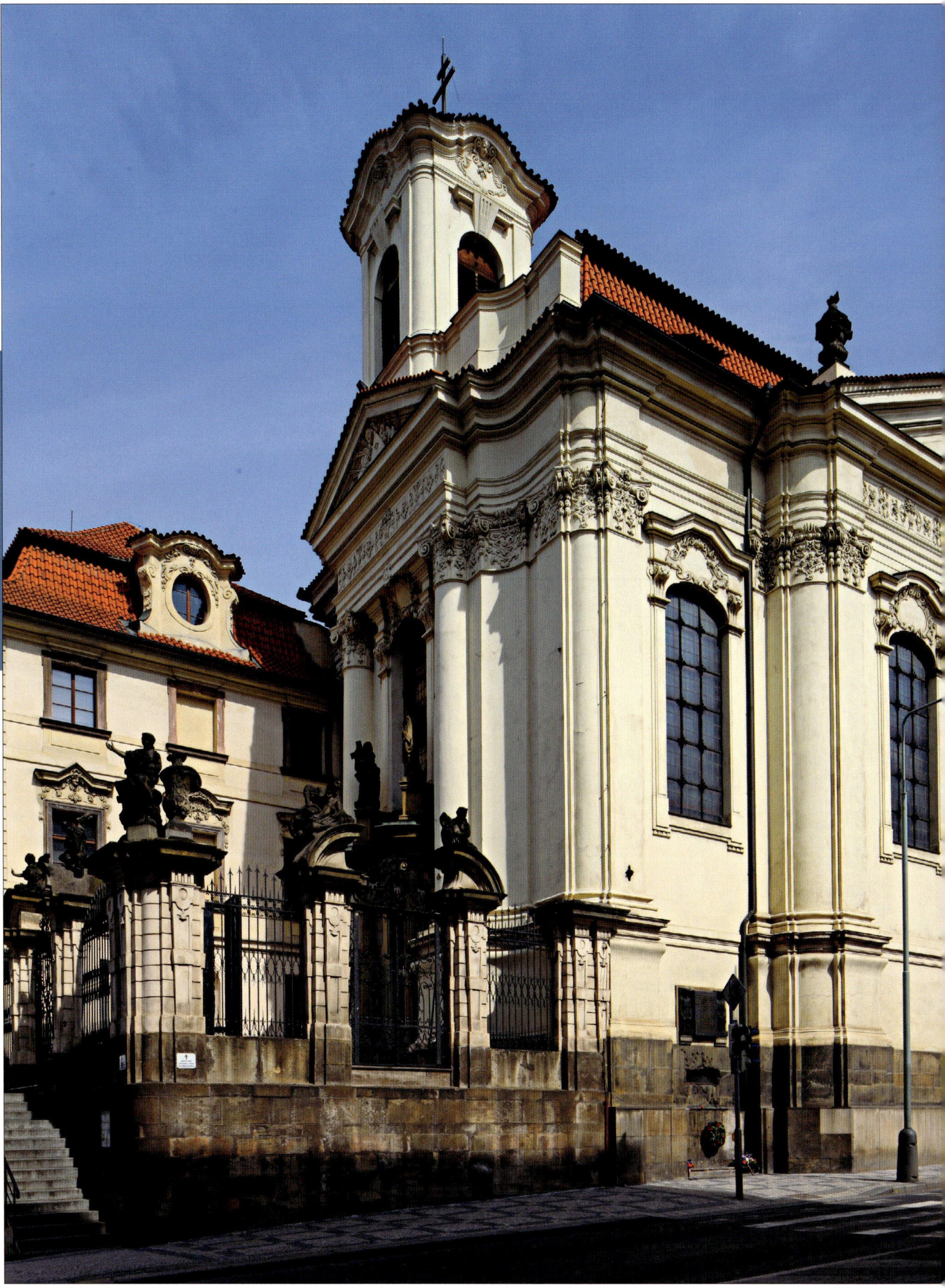

THE CHURCH OF ST. CYRIL AND METHODIUS

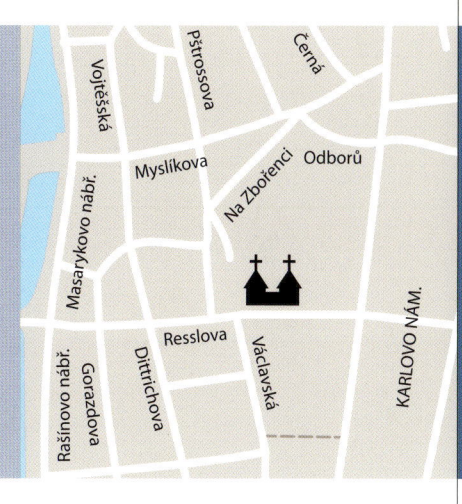

This Baroque Orthodox church was closely joined with the tragic fate of the participants in operation Antropoid, whose peak moment was the 1942 assasination of the Deputy-Reich protector Reinhard Heydrich.

Resslova 307/9a, Prague 2 - New Town

Transport: Metro B Karlovo náměstí, Tram 3, 4, 6, 10, 16, 18, 22, 24 Karlovo náměstí

Worship:
Sun 9:30 am

1730-1736 built
1783 desecrated
1934 passed on to the Czechoslovak Orthodox Church

The Church of St. Cyril and Methodius is easily overlooked, and the thick traffic which has been rerouted here unfortunately forces visitors to Prague to go through this place as quickly as possible. However, architecturally and artistically meaningful sites can be found here, as well as significant sites from the perspective of recent Czech history.

A small church originally stood on the site of what is today the Church of St. Cyril and Methodius; the smaller church was built by Duke Bořivoj I and dedicated to St. Methodius. In exactly this same spot, the first Czech duke and his wife St. Ludmila were said to have been christened by St. Methodius. Around the year 1115, a larger church was built here, the Church of St. Peter and St. Paul; the Crusaders built their Zderaz monastery in the same neighborhood. During the Hussite Wars, however, the church was seriously damaged and gradually fell into ruin. It wasn't until 1705 that the space under Charles Bridge was slowly transformed into its approximate current form. The current Church of St. Cyril and St. Methodius was built from 1730-36 by Pavel Ignác Bayer and Kilián Ignác Dientzenhofer, whose particular artistic style can be seen in many Baroque buildings in Prague.

The church, originally dedicated to Carlo Boromeo, was originally conceived as part of an Emeritus building,

View of the main nave with icons

Picture of St. Wenceslaus and St. Ludmila

designated for overage priests freed from active priestly services on account of their age. This rather sad mission wasn't carried out by the church for long, though. Under the influence of the Josephinian reforms, at the commencement of the issuing of the so-called Tolerance Patent in the year 1781 by Emperor Joseph II, the church was deconsecrated and transformed into a barracks, and in 1866 it was acquired by the Czech Technical University. They used the church for many years as a storage warehouse. Only in 1934 was the church returned to its original purpose and handed over to the use of the Czechoslovakian Orthodox Church. The consecration of the first Orthodox church occurred on the 28th of September, 1935 on the holiday of St. Wenceslas. That didn't last long, however, as the church became the scene of other sad events.

On the 27th of, May 1942 in Libin, Prague, the assassination of the Deputy-Reich protector Reinhard Heydrich was carried out by Josef Gabčík and Jan Kubiš as part of Operation Antropoid. The ensuing wave of Nazi terror, in which the plan was to execute every tenth Czech and which culminated in the burning and murder of the inhabitants of Lidice and Ležáky, had its sad finale in the Church of St. Cyril and Methodius. Right here in the underground crypt, the two assassins and another five paratroopers were hiding. Even today, it is unclear which of the members of this resistance group betrayed the others and led the Gestapo here to the Church of Cyril and Methodius. At four in the morning on the 18th of June, 1942, units of the SS-Waffen and Wehrmacht, consisting of around 800 men, surrounded the church and the adjacent street. After more than two hours of fighting in the church space, during which two of the seriously injured assassins committed suicide, the paratroopers remained barricaded in the underground crypt. The attempts of the SS unit to flood the crypt with water didn't achieve the desired result, and the fate of the defenders, who preferred death by suicide to interrogation by the Gestapo, was only sealed by the penetration through the second opening to the crypt. In the ensuing trials, the first bishop of the Czechoslovakian Hussite (then Orthodox) church, Gorazd, as well as other members of the eparchy

The crypt, where the perpetrators of the assassination of Reinhard Heydrich were hidden. Today there is a National Monument of the heroes of the Heydrichiad here.

of the Orthodox church, were sentenced to death and executed for assisting the assassins. This bloody period of the Second World War entered into Czech cultural and historical consciousness as the so-called Heydrichiad. The church, desecrated by the actions of the Gestapo and the SS unit, was again consecrated on the 5th of July 1947; however, the first post-war mass was administered here before that, on the 13th of May, 1945.

Visitors to the church will be especially intrigued by the opulent Baroque stucco ornamentation by M. I. Palliard and the fresco paintings of K. Schöpf. It's also worth it to check out the wonderfully decorated iconostasis, separating the chancel from the church space with a centrally placed altar. Likewise, the dark-colored biblical motifs on the semi-circular vault provide the church with a unique and ghostly atmosphere, enhanced by its troubled history. A permanent exhibition in the underground crypt is a reminder of the sad role the church played during the Second World War.

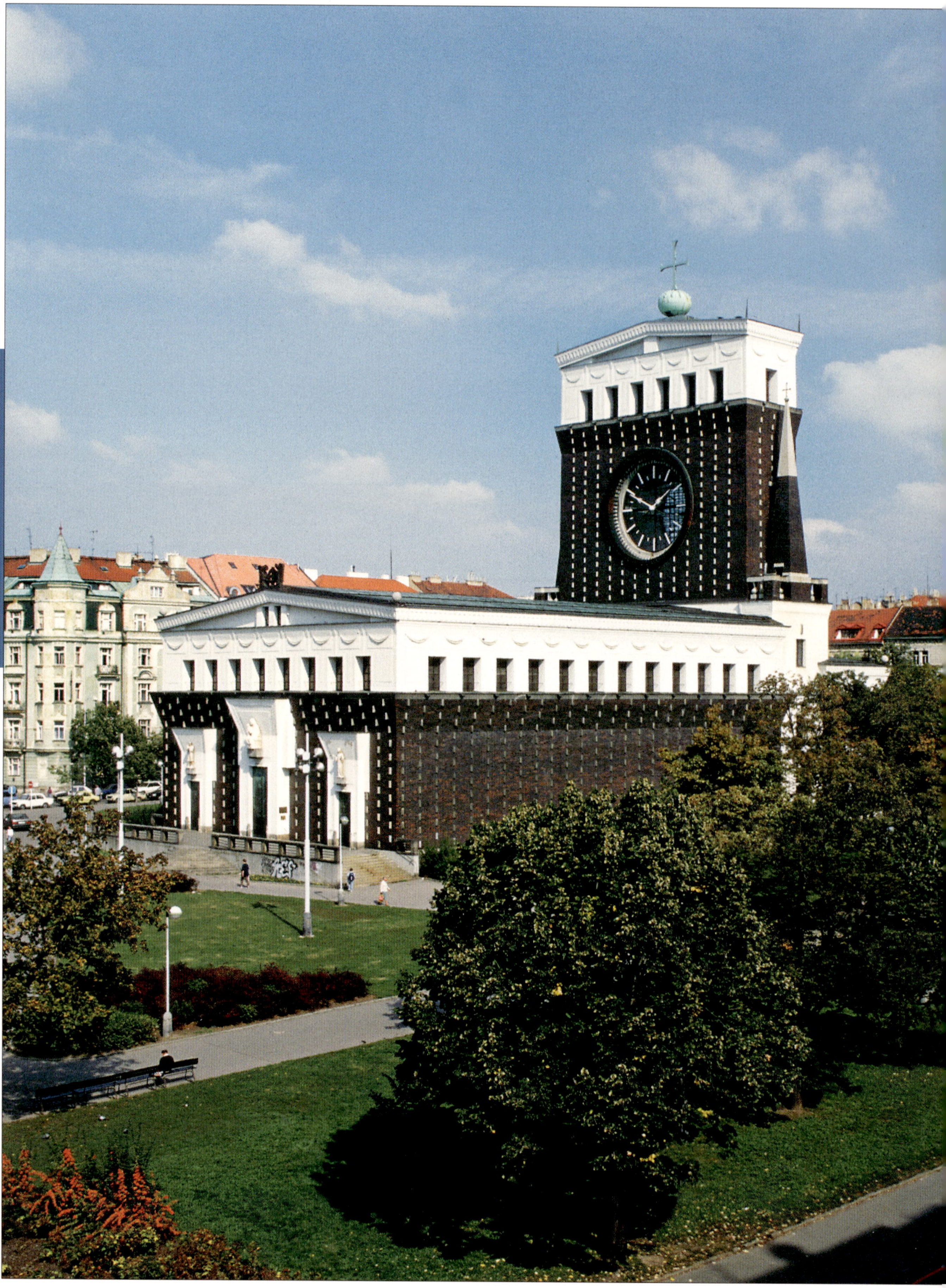

CHURCH OF THE MOST SACRED HEART OF OUR LORD

The most meaningful Czech sacral building of the twentieth century, combining antique elements with avant-garde, geometrically pure architectural design

Jiřího z Poděbrad Square 112/19, Prague 3 - Vinohrady

Transport: Metro A Jiřího z Poděbrad, Tram 11 Jiřího z Poděbrad

Worship:
Mon–Sat 8:00am and 6:00 pm, Sun 9:00 am, 11:00 am, 6:00 pm

1929 construction initiated
1932 construction completed, consecrated

George of Poděbrady Square in Vinohrady is clearly dominated by the most meaningful sacral building of the twentieth century. The giant, almost geometrically shaped church, featuring an enormous glass aperture with a clock in a cuboidal bell tower, is the work of Josip Plečnik. The project itself had a very complicated origin. A society for the construction of churches made the required land available, but the money for the construction itself was missing, and so a design contest was created in the year 1919 for the new sanctuary. Plečnik was contacted as well, but his designs were outside the framework of the competition. In all, he created three very thorough, detailed projects without any financial compensation at all. In the meantime, the authorities freed up the necessary finances; a series of benefactors also contributed money, and a considerable sum was also taken from public collections. On the 28th of October 1928, the tenth anniversary of the creation of an independent Czechoslovakia, art historian and Prague bishop Antonín Podlaha was finally able to lay the founding stone of the future church. Actual construction was initiated on the 26th of August, 1929.

Plečnik, a professor at University of Ljubljana (in today's Slovenia), regularly travelled back and forth to Prague and completed the details and modifications of the growing

Aerial view of George of Poděbrad Square with the Church of the Sacred Heart

General view

▶ View of the interior

church, all for free. In December of 1931, the building site was visited by the Czechoslovak president T. G. Masaryk, who very much respected Plečnik's work. After the end of the First World War, Masaryk named Plečnik the architect of Prague Castle, which he gradually transformed from a decaying and neglected site into a highly presentable presidential compound, combining historical reconstruction with modern architectural elements. Plečnik's distinct style certainly had its critics, who pointed out his perhaps exceedingly avant-garde approach; nevertheless the church, completed and consecrated in May of 1932, reaped universal recognition. The church connects antique elements, particularly visible when viewing the façade, with avant-garde tendencies towards geometrically pure shapes and lines. The outer walls of the temple are formed from glazed bricks for two-thirds of their height, interspersed with white granite blocks. The remaining part of the church aisle is constructed from pure white stones, enclosed in antique moulding. The aisle, which is actually formed from a massive, monolithic block, is optically divided into two parts, each with a different color: the darker and heftier base of glazed bricks forms create a counterpoint to their upper, lighter part, made more intense by their broken moulding, stretching along the perimeter of all four walls. The upper part grows out of the darker base, as if it were gently placed in it. This colorful design spreads out the material of the whole construction, takes the strain off of it and imbues it with a peculiar combination of power and fragility. The fragility is also emphasized by the large, round windows with the clock and the cuboidal design of the bell tower, again finished in antique moulding. We'd like to point out here that there isn't a staircase inside the bell tower, but instead there is an ascending ramp which gradually rises to the top of the tower.

The antique façade is dominated by three portals with statues from the workshop of Bedřich Stefan, created after the Second World War. The interior of the church isn't divided into central and side aisles, but instead forms one large enclosed space. A strictly geometric, pure design in the shape of a cuboid is maintained, which is interrupted by a functionalistically conceived gallery under a flat roof. The interior also combines a dark and light division of the space. At the same time, emphasis is placed on simplicity and maximum ornamental modesty. The walls aren't plastered but are instead built from red, glazed bricks, decorated with small, simple gold crosses. The ceiling is coffered and made from polished wood. The central altar is made from marble and is dominated by a three-meter statue of Christ, made by Damian Pešana out of gilded wood. His hands also crafted the wooden statues of the Czech patrons and saints which are located along the sides of the altar. In the corner of the chancel, sideways from the main altar, there are two smaller altars: an altar of St. Josef on the left side and one to the Virgin Mary on the right side, with statues made by A. Berka. All of the altars were completed after the Second World War; the two altars located near the side wall, the altars of St. Antonin and St. Theresa, are from the protectorate period. These altars had already been designed by Plečnik and were made by Plečnik's successor Otto Rottmayer. Then, from Štěpán Zálešák, we can also see statues of angels. In the avant-garde conceived church, we can also take delight in two wooden Baroque statues from the seventeenth century, which were originally located in the cemetery chapels in Rychnov nad Kněžnou. When the chapel was removed, the statues were transported to the local village hall, where they were forgotten and fell into ruin. The statues were later discovered by a certain married couple, the Šmíd's, who bought them from the village hall. After their death, the statues were inherited by their son, a Vinohrady professor, who gave them to the newly built church on George of Poděbrady Square.

The space beneath the church is also interesting, where an underground crypt, or rather a chapel, can be found. Its victory arch is stone, lined with bricks from the original Romanesque basilica at Prague Castle, which Spytihněv II had built. In the war, the crypt served as an air-raid shelter.

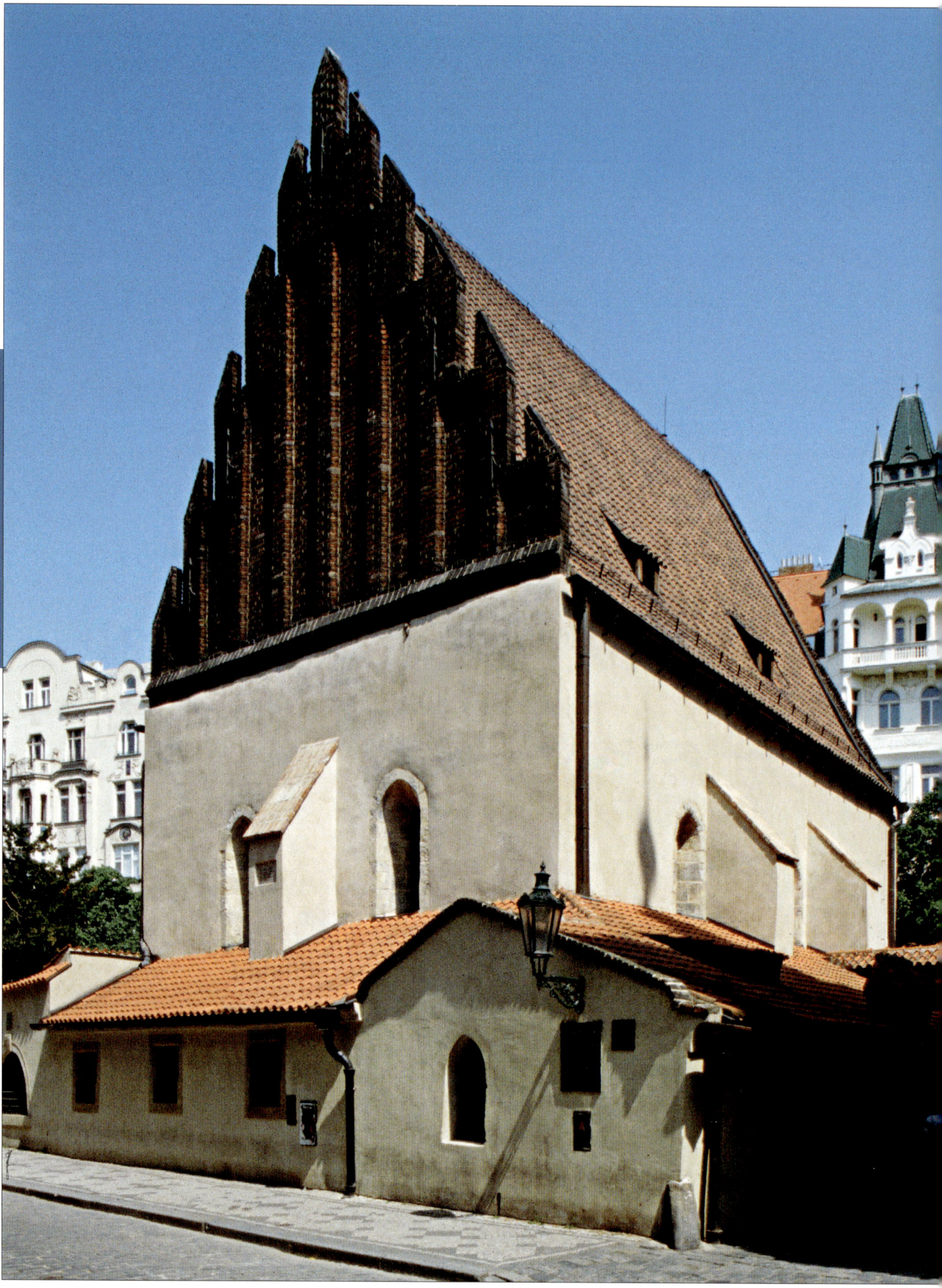

OLD NEW SYNAGOGUE

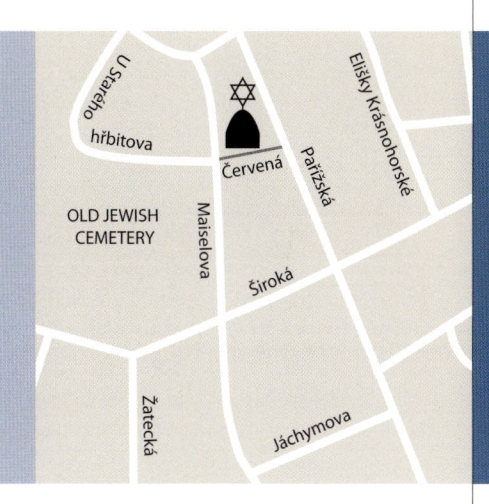

One of the oldest preserved Middle Aged synagogues in Europe, and one of the last remaining buildings of the original Jewish ghetto in Prague

Červená st., Prague 1 - Old Town

Transport: Metro A Staroměstská, Tram 17, 18 Staroměstská

Worship:
regularly, schedule available on the website of the Jewish Community in Prague

Built between 1270-1280

On a small square between Červená, Maiselova and Pařížská Streets, the sagging roof of the Old New synagogue sits, one of the oldest preserved synagogues in Europe and one of the last witnesses of the medieval Jewish ghetto, that labyrinth of distorted street and dark passages which was demolished within the framework of the Prague rehabilitation in the year 1890. The Old New synagogue was established in approximately 1270 to 1280, when the Jewish people living in Prague gained permission from the Czech King, Přemysl Otakar II. The synagogue, which was originally called New or Large Synagogue, was built by royal stonemasons, who were simultaneously working on the construction of a nearby monastery, St. Agnes. The synagogue gained its current name at the end of the sixteenth century, when another synagogue came into existence in the Prague ghetto. However, we might choose to believe a less rational explanation of the name: according to legend, an angel brought stones to Prague to build the synagogue from the demolished Jerusalem church; however, the angel lent the stones only upon the condition that they will be returned once the church is renewed.

The Old New synagogue represents the oldest preserved specimen of a two-aisle Middle Age synagogue. The low, rectangular structure is distinguished by its tall, saddle-like

Old-New Synagogue adjacent to the original Jewish town hall, whose hallmark is a backwards going clock.

roof with its striking, sharp and toothy Gothic gable. The main aisle of the synagogue is encircled by a low building, used as a space for women. The floor of the main aisle is situated deeper than the level of the outer terrain. Descending a few steps down to the middle aisle symbolizes the humiliation of the human psyche and the humility with which human beings appear before the face of God

Two Baroque treasure chests sit in the vestibule in front of the actual sanctuary, in which the tax collected from Jewish people from all over the Czech Kingdom was stored. The entry to the main aisle is formed by a portal, whose tympanum is decorated by a relief of wine leaves and grapes originating from a single bush. This is in reference to the twelve Israeli tribes, growing out of a single root. The same meaning is implied by the twelve narrow windows, which switch upward in six fields of a five-part ribbed vault, consisting of octagonal pillars. The ornamentation of the tympanum and arching bolts is one the most artistically valuable architectural elements of the Old New Synagogue. Their spiritual focal point is naturally the podium in the center of the prayer room (*bimalmemor*) with the elevated place for the reading of the Torah. Its candles are hidden in the tabernacle (*aron ha-kodesh*), facing in the direction of Jerusalem (so on the East side of the synagogue). The sanctuary itself, in front of which an eternal light burns (*ner tamid*), is covered by opulent embroidery and an ornamented curtain (*parokhet*) with draperies. Its aesthetic and artistic imagery symbolizes the demolition of the Temple of Jerusalem. The lighting of the central space is provided by bronze chandeliers from the sixteenth through eighteenth centuries. Another noteworthy artifact is the high, ornamented banner which the Prague Jewish people employed from the end of the fifteenth century. In the middle of the banner we can see the star of David, complemented by a profession of the faith of Sh'ma Israel.

Another interesting item about the Old New synagogue is the original, ornamented wooden seats, which are situated alongside the wall around the perimeter of the sanctuary. One of these, labeled number one, is said to have been used by the legendary Rabbi Löw. The Old New

View of the interior – *bima* (place for reading from the Torah) with a Gothic grille

Rostrum and the Tabernacle

Synagogue always represented the epicenter of the piety of Prague's Jewish people, and therefore the most significant rabbinical figures administered there. In the sixteenth century, for example, Eliezer Ashkenazi, Mordechai ben Abraham Jaffe, Jehuda Löw ben Bezalel, and other well-known rabbis such as Rabbi Löw and the top Prague Rabbi Ezechiel Landau, all came to the Old New synagogue. This is all quite natural, because the Old New Synagogue has been shrouded in a series of myths and legends over the long centuries. Perhaps the most well-known legend is the one about Golem, a creature which could be woken by inserting a small ball into its forehead or mouth. The creator of this demonic being, the reviving ball and the parchment with the magical formula, was Rabbi Jehuda Löw ben Bezalel. By removing the ball, Golem was immobilized. The monster formed out of clay was intended to protect the ghetto from Christian pogroms, and carry out useful work in times of peace. However, one day, during a Jewish holiday, the Rabbi forgot to take the small ball out of Golem. Golem, away from the rabbi, began to destroy his house and threaten the residents of the ghetto. According to one legend, the rabbi subdued the monster at the last moment, took the ball out of its mouth, and Golem collapsed and turned into dust. Another legend indicates that the rotting, clay body of Golem is hidden somewhere in the dark soil of the synagogue.

Perhaps on account of Rabbi Löw's relationship with the Emperor Rudolph II and Tycho de Brahe, with whom he mulled over questions of alchemy, he was known not just for the creation of Golem, but also for his mysticism and secret teachings. The facts (well, those supported by evidence) are that Jehuda Löw worked in Prague as an upper Rabbi. He founded a Talmudistic school (*yeshiva*) and supervised the activities of the Funeral Brethren (*khevra kadisha*). The Prague Maharal, as Löw is called in Jewish documents, now rests in the Jewish cemetery in Prague, under a massive, moss-covered headstone, marked by a statue of a grape vine. Legend says that wishes written on paper and placed into the one of the crevices of the Rabbi's grave will be fulfilled.

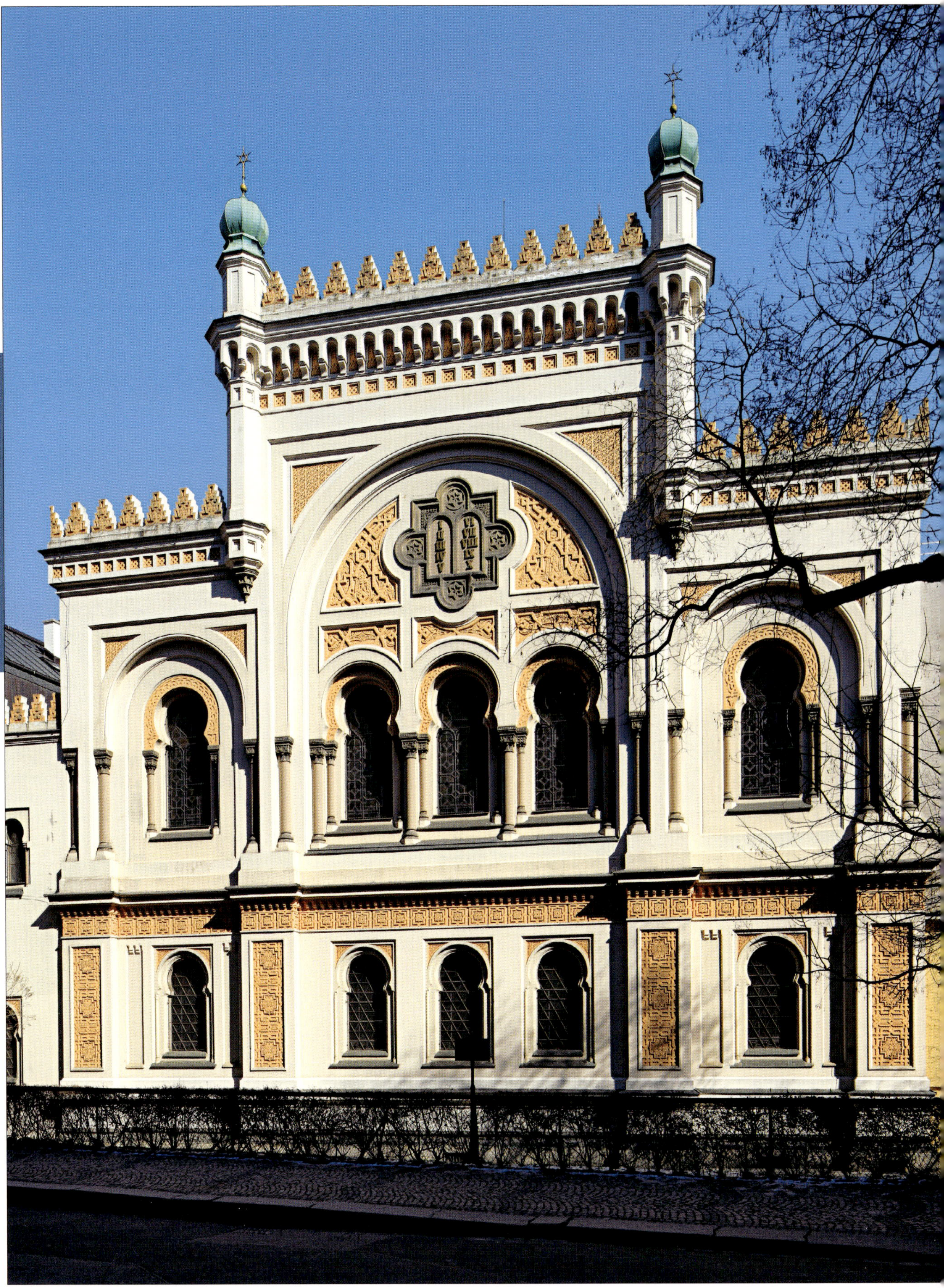

THE SPANISH SYNAGOGUE

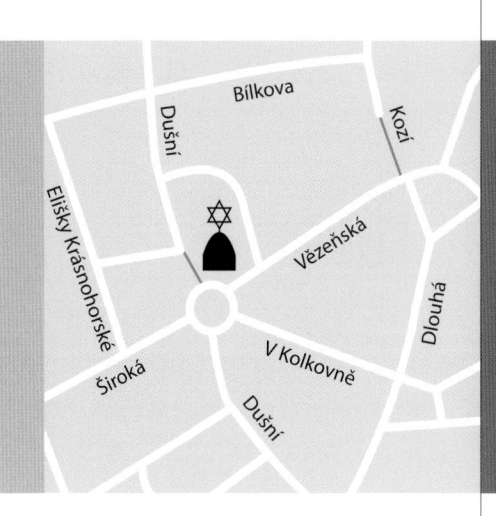

In the interior, a richly ornamented synagogue in a unique Moresque-Islamic style

Vězeňská 141/1, Prague 1 - Old Town

Transport: Metro A Staroměstská, Tram 17, 18 Staroměstská

Worship:
Fri 6:00 pm (Caballa Sabbath)

Built in 1868

During the course of the eleventh and twelfth centuries, Byzantine Jews moved into Prague and settled in the area around what is today Dušní Street. Before the year 1142, the Jews had already built the oldest Jewish temple in Prague, called Old School (*Altschul*), after the original prayer room in Lesser Town had burned down. The ghetto which came into being around Old School never merged with the ghetto at the Old New Synagogue, and so two Jewish constituencies existed next to each other, later separated by the Catholic Church of St. Ducha. The fate of Old School was not an easy one: during the anti-Jewish pogroms in 1389, 1516, 1604 and 1622, the temple was demolished, set on fire, and looted several times. In 1744, when a decree from Marie Theresa expelled Jews from the Czech Republic for the crime of alleged cooperation with the Prussians, the Old School ceased to be maintained. The Jews weren't allowed to return until four years later.

At the beginning of the nineteenth century, the Old School became Prague's center of the German speaking reformist Jews, and in 1837, a reform church service was implemented here. It's also interesting that from 1836-45, František Škroup, author of the musical national anthem *Where My Home Is*, played the organ here. The unsuitable technical state of the Old School and its shoddy neo-Gothic

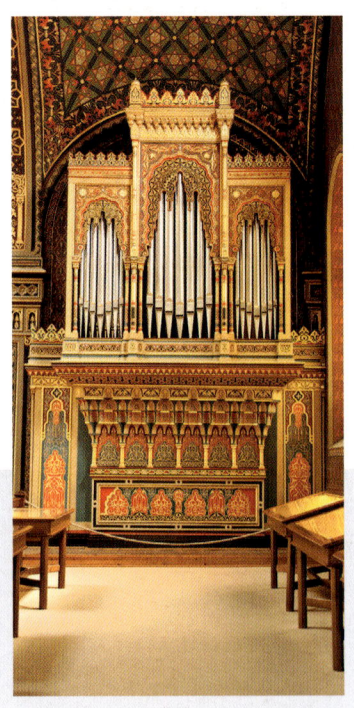

Main hall, view to the east wall with the sanctuary

In The Spanish Synagogue Franz Škroup, composer of the Czech national anthem *Where is my home*, served as organist.

➤ The eastern wall with the sanctuary (*aron ha-kodesh*) and stained glass in the form of six-pointed stars

reconstruction eventually led to the decision to demolish the original sanctuary and build a new, more extensive synagogue in the popular Moresque architectural style. Design for the new building was entrusted to Ignác Ullmann. The interior design was assigned to Josef Niklas, a representative of the historical style. The new synagogue buildings were completed in 1868.

The actual layout of the synagogue is formed from a one-storey building with a square floor plan in the main hall, which is complemented on three sides by a neo-Renaissance gallery. The central space of the synagogue is enclosed above by a richly ornamented Moresque-style cupola, which also matches the stucco, gilded and multicolored arabesque, reminiscent of Islamic decorative arts. The richly gilded, ornamental decoration, with its architectural and aesthetic connection to the interior design of a similar sanctuary in Andalusian Alhambra, earned the synagogue its Spanish title.

The Spanish Synagogue continued in the reform tradition, which commenced in the Old School at the beginning of the nineteenth century. Visitors will recognize this tendency in the placement of the so-called *bima*, the raised space for the reading of the Torah, which isn't situated in the middle of the synagogue, but on its east wall. Likewise, the benches for believers are organized in an untraditional manner, similar to Christian churches.

The Old New Synagogue was used for worship up until the Second World War; however, it was taken over in the mid-1950s by the Jewish museum, which gradually focused on a unique, permanent exposition of synagogal textiles, from draperies to synagogal curtains as well as the casing of Torah candles. The exposition, which also represents the history of Jewish people in the Czech territory and exhibits features examples of silver artwork, features textile relics from the Renaissance up until the present. Classical concerts also take place in the Spanish Synagogue.

131

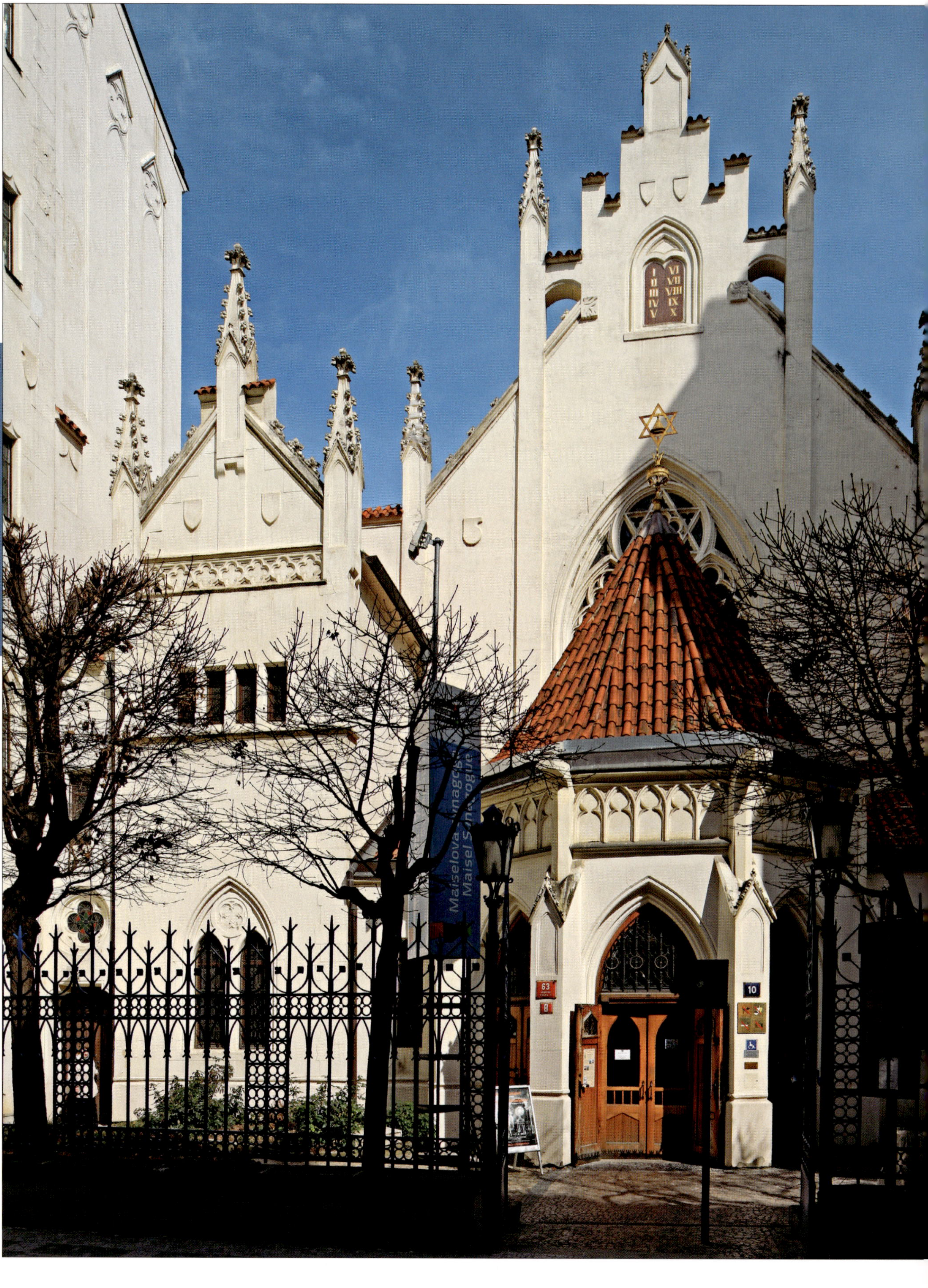
Maiselova
Maisel
10
63

MAISEL SYNAGOGUE

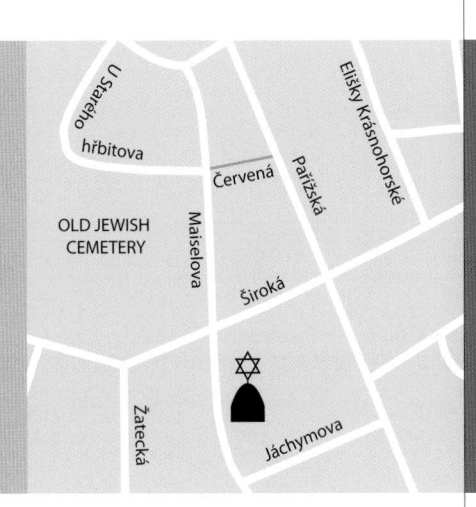

A reconstructed, neo-Gothic-style synagogue with an extensive exhibition, familiarizing visitors with the development of Jewish settlements in Bohemian and Moravian lands and representing precious synagogal objects from the workshops of Jewish goldsmiths and metalsmiths

Maiselova 10, Prague 1 - Old Town
Transport: Metro A Staroměstská, Tram 17, 18 Staroměstská
Worship:
none
Built in 1592
1689 rebuilt in the Baroque style
1893-1905 Gothic reconstruction

Only five synagogues survived the historically controversial reconstruction of the Old Town section of Prague, among them Maisel synagogue, from the end of the sixteenth century. Mordechai ben Samuel Maisel had it built, having bought a neglected parcel of land with a decaying home in the ghetto in the year 1590. Emperor Rudolph II granted Maisel permission to build the synagogue in 1591, and the new synagogue was already consecrated within a year, on the 30th of September 1592.

Maisel was one of the richest men in the Czech kingdom in his time and he administered the Jewish ghetto. Due to his wealth, Maisel had significant influence on the society of that time, as well as political happenings in the Prague under Rudolph II. He loaned money to Czech nobles, financed some of the Emperor's war ventures, and he also helped Rudolph acquire a costly art collection for Prague Castle. He improved the Jewish ghetto with money from his own pocket, having new pavement laid throughout the entire ghetto. He founded several spas and clinics, expanded the Jewish cemetery, and paid for the construction of two synagogues and a Jewish town hall. And that's not all: with his money and indisputable diplomatic skills he obtained and purchased many privileges and liberties for the Jewish people of Prague.

The synagogue, whose construction was funded by Maisel, was designed as a three-aisle Renaissance sanctuary with two portals. Josef Wahl and Juda Goldsmied de Herz were hired to do the building. The large fire of Old Town, set by French agents in June of 1689, was dodged by Maisel's synagogue, escaping with only a singed roof. During its repair, the synagogue acquired some Baroque features. A second fire in 1754 damaged the building more significantly. However, the synagogue was quickly repaired and its Renaissance form was more or less respected during the process. Neo-Gothic repairs commenced only at the end of the nineteenth century, in accordance with a project by A. Grott, which removed a few valuable historic and artistic architectural elements. The modifications affected both the interior, where the podium (*almemor*) was destroyed for deaconing, and later the compartment for the Torah and other sacral objects (*aron ha-kodesh*) were modified in a Neogothic style; of course, the exterior was also affected. In the year 1894, the annex on the west side of the synagogue was demolished and the façade acquired a jagged neo-Gothic form with plates of the Ten Commandments placed high in the points of the façade peak with a bent Gothic bulge. Under them, we can see tall, neo-Gothic-style windows in whose peak there is a six-pointed Jewish star. A three-sided vestibule is set in the façade, reminiscent of late Gothic churches. Entry to the synagogue is through a small garden, which somewhat lightens the whole space; after the rehabilitation of the ghetto, the synagogue found itself literally wedged between two large town-houses, which gives the overall layout of the building an unbalanced feel. The interior of the synagogue is designed as a three-aisle building with low and narrow and low. From the original Renaissance form, only the supporting pillars of the side wall and the female gallery upstairs remain.

During the war, the synagogue was used as a warehouse for confiscated Jewish property, and now there is currently an exposition in the synagogue on the history of Jews in Bohemia and Moravia. In the central aisle, we can be acquainted with the beginnings of Jewish settlements in the Czech territory. In the middle of the aisle an exposition of Jewish synagogal silver objects is located. The exposition also shows a parchment code from the fifteenth century, outlining the privileges provided to the Jews by Přemysl Otakar II and Charles IV. It's also definitely worth taking a look at a bill of debt from the year 1378, on which Jan Žižka from Trocnov, leader of the Hussite army, is signed as a guarantor. In another showcase, there is material dedicated to significant Jewish scholars and rabbis from the twelfth to the eighteenth centuries. We should also note the precious manuscript of the Pentateuch from the year 1530.

If we move from the central to the south aisle, we can be acquainted with the development of Jewish settlements in Bohemia and Moravia, complemented by Jewish documents. Objects connected to key Jewish figures from Prague are displayed in the north aisle. Here we can admire the gilded cup of Rabbi Löw or the gold and silver covered crown on the Torah from the year 1783. Another unique object is the guild symbol of the Prague Butcher's Guild, taking the form of a key, from the year 1620; we can also admire engravings from the years 1716 and 1741, depicting processions of Jewish residents of Prague. The exposition concludes with documents from the reign of Marie Theresa when, after a long period of expulsion from Prague, the position of Jewish people improved and they were able to return again.

Neo-Gothic facade with slabs of the ten Commandments

135

... FINALLY, A FEW MORE STEPS THROUGH PRAGUE

Our survey of Prague's churches, temples and synagogues is necessarily limited regarding the number of sacred buildings in the territory of Prague, as well as with regard to the size of this volume. Our selection has in fact omitted dozens of other interesting sacred buildings. Likewise, the legends, myths, and descriptions of the forementioned sights are certainly not exhaustive; it is merely a basic probe, the thorough examination of which requires different and more specialized literature. This is why we have enclosed a list of several other sacred buildings for the reader - although certainly not an exhaustive one - which could not be given individual chapters, but which should not be overlooked by the architecture- and art-loving pilgrim wandering through Prague ...

Let us begin our pilgrimage near St. Vitus Cathedral in Hradčany Square. If we set off from its northern edge around the Marian plague column, which the grateful people of Prague erected between 1724 and 1736 in thanks for the end of the plague outbreak, the slim and somehow twisted Kanovnická Street opens for us. Following the street leads us to the Baroque **Church of St. John of Nepomuk**, built between 1720 and 1729, close to the monastery of Ursulines. The church, romantically wedged into a sloping ground formed by the streets Kanovnická and U Kasáren, is probably the first sacred building designed by Kilián Ignác Dienzenhofer. In a richly decorated interior, what attracts one's attention is mainly the magnificent illusory ceiling painting by V. V. Reiner, who chose the theme of the apotheosis of St. John of Nepomuk. If we set off further down the lane U Kasáren and go down the street of Nový Svět, and then clamber up again over the bumpy pavement of Černínská Street, on the right we will see an early Baroque **Church of the Virgin Mary of Angels**, built around 1600 as a part of the grounds of the former Capuchin monastery, which is a neighbour of Loreta. From Loreta through Pohořelec it is only a little way to the **Church of the Assumption of the Virgin Mary, located near the** Strahov monastery. In the first half of the 12th century, when the first friars of the Order of the Premonstratensians began to settle here, there were deep, deserted forests, and old chronicles remind us that in the long and dark winters, hungry wolves sneaked through these places towards the gates of Prague Castle. The Premonstratensians gradually cut down the forests, and in 1143 they started work on a stone monastery complex, next to which there also grew a majestic, three-aisle Romanesque basilica with a pair of prismatic towers. After some time, a Gothic transept was added. The temple that had been decaying for decades after the Hussite looting was renovated at the end of the sixteenth century, when it was restored in the Renaissance spirit. During the Swedish siege of Prague at the end of the Thirty Years' War, the monastery complex was looted once again, and the Swedish troops took everything that had any value: statues, paintings, art objects, almost the whole library and half a million of golden pieces. At the turn of the eighteenth century, the monastery area with its church acquired a Baroque feel, but the temple suffered badly once more; this time it was due to the Austrian artillery that had Prague under siege, which was then taken over by the French. After the subsequent repairs, overseen by an architect named Anselmo Lurago, the temple acquired the Baroque style that it still has today. Inside the temple, we can admire many wonderful scuptures and paintings, whether a twelve-part cycle of frescos from the life of St. Norbert, or eight great ceiling paintings depicting scenes from the life of the Virgin Mary. Once in the Strahovský courtyard, let us pause at the Gothic-Renaissance **Church of St. Roch**, which was protected by its patron against the Black Death. It was built between 1603 and 1612 with the costs covered by Rudolf II., on the site where the Chapel of St. Eberhard had stood since 1316, but had been destroyed during the Hussite Wars. The Church of St. Roch is empty and deconsecrated today, and serves mostly as an exhibition hall.

From the Strahovský monastery we can walk down Úvoz and then Nerudova Streets to Malostranské Square and thence, through a darkened passageway, we can get to Letenská Street. On the left is **St Thomas' Church**, originally a Gothic three-aisle temple, built between 1285 and 1379 near the monastery of the Augustinians. The church was burned down during the Hussite Wars, restored in the Renaissance style in the middle of the sixteenth century, and rebuilt in a Baroque style between 1727 and 1731. If our steps lead the opposite way, toward Kampa, we will go round the Čertovka Ravine (Devil's Channel) to the end of the park, where Říční Street begins. On the corner, we can see a small chapel. In fact, it is the **Church of Saint John the Baptiste Na Prádle**, a one-aisle, Romanesque-Gothic church built around 1240. At the beginning of the eighteenth century the church was partly renovated in a Baroque style, probably by K. I. Dienzenhofer. The space in front of the sanctuary is decorated by the baroque sculpture of St. John of Nepomuk, created by M. J. Brokoff in 1715.

Then we can go back and over Charles Bridge to the right bank of Vltava, to the lanes of Old Town. From the arbour of the bridge tower there emerges in front of us the bulky Baroque facade of the **Church of the Holiest Salvator**, one of the most significant Baroque sights of Prague, the part of the Jesuit hall of residence, Klementinum. The Jesuits came to Prague in 1556, invited by Ferdinand I., and their task was to create a cultural, spiritual, and intellectual background for the Habsburg re-Catholicization of the Czech lands. A vast monastery complex had already been built there by Dominicans around 1230. However, it did not survive the looting of the Hussites, and the entire site was dilapidated until the time when a great Jesuit area began to develop. The building of the temple, which had partly grown on the foundations of the older Gothic St. Clement's Church, began in 1578, probably based on the drawings of Giovanni Fontano di Brusata (even though

Carlo Luragho is often cited as their author). Construction of the bulky temple took almost a hundred and sixty years. In its interior, we can admire a beautiful stucco decoration from the middle of the seventeenth century, a ceiling mural in the chancel created around 1748 and depicting four continents (Australia was still waiting to be discovered), the painting of Ignác and St. František Xaverský by the central altar, or the confessionals, whose pictures of the Apostles show the sculpting mastery of J. J. Bendl. Its statues decorated the facade of the temple in 1660. The top of the frontal buckler is dominated by the statue of the Saviour of the World, with the apostles Luke and John to the left, and Matthew and Mark to the right. There is a statue of the Virgin Mary in the niche under the shield, and an advance balustrade is supplied by the statues of St. Clement, Augustine, Pope George V., St. Ambrose, Jerome, and Adalbert.

In the maze of Old Town's streets, at the intersection of Liliová and Zlatá streets, we should not pass by without noticing the dismal, blackened **St. Anna's Church**. It is a one-aisle Gothic monastery church, built between 1319 and 1330 on the site of an original Romanesque rotunda from the twelfth century, strangely hidden in a blind alleyway from the curious glances and the chaotic looks Old Town's residents and visitors. Its facade is hidden in the second courtyard of the former convent of the Dominican Sisters, and a pilgrim will actually catch only a glimpse of the gloomy end of the temple that had been deconsecrated a long time ago. The Knights Templar may have settled there around 1232, but after the abolishment of their order in 1312 and the burning of the grand master Jacob de Molay, the temple was given to the Knights of St. John, who sold it to the Dominican Sisters the following year. They lived here until 1782, when the Dominican monastery with its neighbouring church became victims of the reforma-

tions of Joseph II. It then became a book and paper storage room, while in the adjacent areas of the abandoned monastery there developed stores for the National Theatre... The Church of St. Anna found its true calling in 1997, when its reconstruction became a part of a project of the former president Václav Havel and his wife Dagmar, called VIZE 97. In 2004, the Church of St. Anna entered the world of knowledge as a so-called Prague crossroads, a cultural and spiritual center and meeting place, following the message of the ex-president Havel.

If we go back towards Old Town Square, we cannot miss a the wide steps of the Baroque **Temple of St. Nicholas** from the eighteenth century, built on the basis of a project by Kilián Ignác Dienzenhofer. Its exterior is decorated with statues created by Antonín Braun, a nephew of Matyáš Bernard Braun; inside, our attention is caught by the stuccos of B. Spinetti, and also by the famous crystal chandelier, built in 1880 by Harrach glassworks as a gift to the Russian tsar, from the time when the temple of St. Nicholas served all the believers.

At the intersection of Malá Štupartská and Jakubská streets emerges the second oldest Prague temple after St. Vitus' Cathedral, **the Church of Jacob the Greater**. Its origin dates back to 1232, when Vitus I called minorities and smaller brothers of the Franciscans to Prague, and began constructing the church and the monastery. In 1316, the nearby Jewish ghetto went up in flames, and the flames hit the monastery complex as well. In 1319, a new temple was built on the impulse of John the Blind, which grew to the shape of a three-aisle basilica. During the Hussite Wars, the temple was allegedly protected against the Utraquists by the butchers of the Old Town.

In 1689, the temple was burned completely to the ground due to a massive fire in Old Town, and after the subsequent repair by John Šimon Pánka, it gained the Baroque style which it has today. From the Church of St. James the Greater, it is not far to the **Church of St. Salvator** by the Anežský convent, finished in 1265 in a light French Gothic style. The Church of St. Salvator is closely connected to Anežka Přemyslovna, better known as St. Agnes of Bohemia, who wanted to make an industrial graveyard out of the temple of St. Salvator. The following church is also devoted to the Saviour of the World; it is Prague's largest evangelic **temple, U Salvátora**. Construction on the original church began in 1611 and in three years it was consecrated, but it had to wait for the facade to be finished. The temple grew into a Gothic-Renaissance basilica, and was remade in a Baroque style after the great Old Town fire in 1689.

But here we are again in the maze of the Old Town alleys, where we should pause at Pinkas' Synagogue, which now serves as a Holocaust memorial. **Pinkas' Synagogue** actually grew out of the impulse of the ancestry of Horovic, who did not approve of the Old New synagogue. So in the second half of the fifteenth century, Pinkas Aron Mešuliam Horovic, called Pinkas the Mouthy, set out to construct his own synagogue. Another significant Prague synagogue is the **Klausová synagogue**, situated near the entrance to the Jewish graveyard, and named after three buildings - klauses - in Renaissance style. During the great Old Town fire of 1689, klauses burned down and many Jews died in the flames. In 1694, a contemporary synagogue was built there. We can also pause at a number of other sacral buildings, like at the baroque **Church of St. Michael**, wedged into a small site by Melantrichova and Michalská Streets. There had originally been a Romanesque church on that site, probably built thanks to Peter Berka from Dubá, who was the Grand Master of the Knights Templar. In the middle of the fourteenth century the church succumbed to the Gothic three-naval temple, which was rebuilt in a Baroque style in the middle of the seventeenth century by brothers of the Order of Servitudes. Today, one can find multimedia shows of a strange nature... Our steps, therefore, lead away and to the New Town area of Prague.

Among the most magnificent sacral buildings of New Town is surely the Jesuit **Church of St. Ignaz** from Loyola on the crossroads of Charles' Square and Ječná Street, built between 1665 and 1670 in the early Baroque style by Carl Luragho. In the end of the seventeenth century the church gained a balconied portico, a somewhat open entrance hall. In the peaceful, silent space of the church we can admire a Classicist central altar from the eighteenth century with the painting *Celebration of St. Ignaz*, which was painted in 1687 by J. J. Heinsch. If we clamber up the alleys to the right of the Church of St. Ignaz, we will come to the Church of St. Apollinaris, founded in the middle of the fourteenth century by Charles IV. He chose the highest point of the planned New Town, called Větrov, for the site of this church. A small Gothic church with one naval, which is supplemented by eight-sided towers, was consecrated in 1363. The church, easily overlooked on the narrow, sharply sloping, Apollinaris (Apolinářská) Street, has a strangely romantic atmosphere, which is emphasized by the fact that the place is usually deserted. In the interior of **the Church of St. Apollinaris** we can spot Gothic frescos in good condition, made around 1390, or the painting of the Virgin Mary of Karlov from the master J. J. Heinsch. The Baroque painting, created in 1697, is a part of the altar with the same name from 1740, and is interesting by virtue of its unique theme - it depicts the pregnant Virgin Mary. The painting was ascribed magical power and pregnant women used to kneel in prayers in front of it to pray for a successful delivery of their child.

The journey in search for other extraordinary churches and temples will lead us to various directions and various parts of Prague. Peace Square in Vinohrady is dominated by **the Church of St. Ludmila**, a monumental, neo-Gothic, monumental, three-naval brick basilica, built between 1888 and 1892 based on a project by Josef Mocker. From Královské Vinohrady we can go down to the streets of Žižkov to Sladkovského Square, the central point of which is also a neo-Gothic, three-aisle **Temple of St. Prokop**. TThe temple's facade is dominated by a seventy-meter-high tower. The church, which was built here between 1899 and 1903, carries the mark of Josef Mocker and is slightly reminiscent of a diminished variant of the Church of St. Ludmila of Vinohrady. The **Church of St. Cyril and Methodius** also demonstrates a certain fashionable historical architecture as well; it is a massive, three-aisle basilica built in a formerly industrial zone in a neo-Romanesque style between 1854 and 1863, and based on a project by Karl Rössner and Ignác Ullmann. The temple is dominated by its monumental facade with a lancet stellar window. The almost oppressive mightiness of the construction is lightened by a pair of tall, slender towers that loom over Karlin. The last sacral building born by the historicizing style in architecture is the neo-Gothic **Temple of St. Antonín of Padua** in Holešovice. It was built on the basis of a project by František Mikša, a pupil of Josef Mocker, on the site of a former cycling track. The first cornerstone was laid in 1908, and despite some financial trouble, construction was finished and the church was consecrated in 1911. The church is a three-aisle temple, the facade of which is dominated by a pair of tall towers located on both sides of the portal.

Conversely, in answer to the wave of neo-Gothic and neo-Romanesque architecture, we can look at **St. Vitus' Church** at the Vršovický Square of Svatopluk Čech, a remarkable, functional building of clean, geometric lines, built between 1929 and 1930 by Josef Gočár. The colorful front window was designed by Josef Kaplický. Moving on, we will be brought back to the times when Vršovice consisted merely of country houses, spreading through the hilly country to the vineyards, by the romantic, Baroque **Church of St. Nicholas** in Vršovické Square. Sitting in the midst of huge, modern apartment buildings, the church seems almost inappropriate, like a scene from old postcards. The one-naval church, built in 1704 and extended between 1894 and 1896, was preceded by a sacral Gothic building and this was probably preceded by a smaller sanctuary from the eleventh century.

It has already been noted that this publication is limited in its presentation of Prague's sacred sites; it is not a specialized, scientific discourse or an encyclopaedic list of the best. This book aims to encourage readers to go beyond superficial visits to the great and well-known churches which are described in every tired tourist guide, and to explore the secret places that are hidden in gardens, deserted alleys, or on the peripheries of the busy streets of Prague.

Church of St Nicholas in the Lesser Town

141

SOURCES

Bedrníček, Pavel:
Příběhy pražských svatyní. Praha, Volvox Globator 2009.

Bělina, Pavel a kol.:
Dějiny Prahy I.: Od nejstarších dob do sloučení pražských měst (1784). Praha - Litomyšl, Paseka 1997.

Bělina, Pavel a kol.:
Dějiny Prahy II.: Od sloučení pražských měst v roce 1784 do současnosti. Praha - Litomyšl, Paseka 1998.

Bělina, Pavel a kol.:
Dějiny zemí Koruny české II.: Od nástupu osvícenství po naši dobu. Praha - Litomyšl, Paseka 2002.

Cibula, Václav:
Pražské pověsti. Praha, Orbis 1972.

Čornej, Petr a kol.:
Dějiny zemí Koruny české I.: Od příchodu Slovanů do roku 1740. Praha - Litomyšl, Paseka 2002.

Dudák, Vladislav:
Pražský poutník aneb Prahou ze všech stran. Praha, Baset 1997.

Dvořák, Tomáš a kol.:
Žižkov: Svéráz pavlačí a strmých ulic. Praha, Muzeum hlavního města Prahy 2012.

Herout, Jaroslav:
Prahou deseti staletí: Přehled stavebních slohů. Praha, Orbis 1972.

Horák, Jiří:
Kniha o staré Praze. Praha, Mladá fronta 1998.

Chalupa, Karel:
Z tajů pražských pověstí. Praha, Drahomíra Sladká 1946.

Kašička, František; Nechvátal, Bořivoj:
Vyšehrad pohledem věků. Praha, Správa národní kulturní památky Vyšehrad 1985.

Katedrála sv. Víta, ed. Merhautová, Anežka a kol. autorů. Praha, Academia 1994.

Košnář, Julius:
Staropražské pověsti a legendy. Praha, Odeon 1992.

Krejčí, Karel:
Praha legend a skutečností. Praha, Panorama 1981.

Krejčí, Karel:
Podivuhodné příběhy ze staré Prahy. Praha, Odeon 1971.

Langer, František:
Pražské legendy. Praha, Albatros 2000.

Lazarová, Markéta: *Praha: Obraz města v 16. a 17. století.* Praha, Argo - Schola ludus - Pragensia 2002.

Lorenc, Vilém:
Nové Město pražské. Praha, SNTL 1973.

Míka, Zdeněk: *Karlín: Nejstarší předměstí Prahy.* Praha, Muzeum hlavního města Prahy 2011.

Přemyslovský stát kolem roku 1000, eds. Polanský, Luboš; Sláma, Jiří; Třeštík, Dušan. Praha, NLN 2000.

Ravik, Slavomír: *Velká kniha o Praze.* Praha, Regia - Knižní klub 2000.

Státníková, Pavla:
Vinohrady: Dobrá čtvrť pro dobré bydlení. Praha, Muzeum hlavního města Prahy 2012.

Škoda, Eduard:
Pražské svatyně. Praha, Libri 2002.

Tomek, Václav Vladivoj:
Pražské židovské pověsti a legendy. Praha, Volvox Globator 2007.

Vlček, Pavel a kol.:
Umělecké památky Prahy: Staré Město, Josefov. Praha, Academia 1996.

Vlček, Pavel a kol.:
Umělecké památky Prahy: Pražský hrad a Hradčany. Praha, Academia 2000.

Vlček, Pavel a kol.:
Umělecké památky Prahy: Malá Strana. Praha, Academia 1999.

Wenig, Adolf:
Staré pověsti pražské. Praha, Josef Hokr 1937.

ILLUSTRATIONS & PHOTO CREDITS

Page 2: St. Vitus Cathedral, the main façade. Photo © Roman Maleček

Page 10: St. Vitus Cathedral, view from the 3rd Courtyard of Prague Castle. Photo © Roman Maleček

Page 12: Prague Castle with St. Vitus Cathedral, view from Strahov. Photo © Roman Maleček

Page 13: Prague Castle with St. Vitus Cathedral. Photo © Jan Rendek

Page 14 left: Hradčanské Square, The new royal palace, 1st and 2nd courtyard of Prague Castle. Photo © Jan Rendek

Page 14 right: The Cathedral of St. Vitus, a view of the main nave. Photo © Jan Rendek

Page 15: The Cathedral of St. Vitus, chancel with the mausoleum of the Habsburgs. Photo © Jan Rendek

Page 16: 1st courtyard of Prague Castle, the New Royal Palace and Cathedral of St. Vitus. Photo © Roman Maleček

Page 17 top: St. Vitus Cathedral, view from St. George's Monastery. Photo © Roman Maleček

Page 17 bottom: St. Vitus Cathedral, the main façade. Photo © Roman Maleček

Page 18: St George's Basilica, view of the main façade. Photo © Roman Maleček

Page 20: St. George's Basilica, general view from the Cathedral of St. Vitus. Photo © Roman Maleček

Page 21: The Square by St. George's. Photo © Roman Maleček

Page 22: Loretta, the façade building with a bell tower. Photo © Roman Maleček

Page 24 left: Loreta chimes. Photo © Roman Maleček

Page 24 right: Loretta, view of the façade building. Photo © Roman Maleček

Page 25: Spring mood at Loreta Square. Photo © Roman Maleček

Page 26-27: Aerial view of Loreta. Photo © Jan Rendek

Page 28: The Church of Peter and Paul, view from the Vltava. Photo © Roman Maleček

Page 30 left: View of the church of St Peter and Paul from the Vyšehrad orchards. Photo © Roman Maleček

Page 30 right: The church of Peter and Paul with Vyšehrad rock. Photo © Roman Maleček

Page 31: The Neo-Gothic tympanum in the facade of the church of St Peter and Paul with a motif of the Last Judgment by S. Zálešák (1902). Photo © Roman Maleček

Page 32: View of the interior of the church of St Peter and Paul. Photo © Zdeněk Thoma

Page 33 left: The entry portals with a mosaic by L. Šindelář. Photo © Roman Maleček

Page 33 right: The capitular Church of St. Peter and Paul, the west facade before re-gothization (B. Roubalik, before 1885). Washed pen drawing. MMP 27.292

Page 34 (3 pictures): Decorative neo-Gothic chapiter under the supporting ribs of the presbytery arch. Photo © Roman Maleček

Page 35: The panorama of Vyšehrad. Photo © Roman Maleček

Page 36: St Martin's Rotunda. Photo © Roman Maleček

Page 38-39: St Martin's Rotunda with surrounding park area. Photo © Roman Maleček

Page 39: The Rotunda of St. Martin in a line drawing by B. Havránek. MMP 33.683

Page 40: Church of the Virgin Mary under the Chain, general view. Photo © Roman Maleček

Page 42 left: Church of the Virgin Mary under the Chain, close up of the gate. Photo © Roman Maleček

Page 42 right: Church of the Virgin Mary under the Chain, iew of the main nave and the altar. Photo © Roman Maleček

Page 43: A pair of towers of the Church of the Virgin Mary under the Chain with the panorama of the Smetana and Masaryk embankment and the National Theatre. Photo © Roman Maleček

Page 44: Church of Our Lady of Victory, general view. Photo © Roman Maleček

Page 46: Aerial view of the church of Our Lady Victorious with Karmelitská Street. Photo © Jan Rendek

Page 47 left: Church of Our Lady Victorious with Prague Castle in the background. Photo © Jan Rendek

Page 47 right: View of the main façade from Karmelitská street . Photo © Roman Maleček

Page 48: Statue of the Infant Jesus. Photo © Jan Rendek

Page 48-49: Church of Our Lady Victorious, view of the main nave. Photo © Roman Maleček

Page 50: View of the Týn church from Old Town Square with the staircase of the Hus monument in the foreground. Photo © Roman Maleček

Page 52-53: View of Old Town Square with Týn Church. Photo © Roman Maleček

Page 54: The main altar with an image of the Assumption of the Virgin Mary by Karel Škréta. Photo © Zdeněk Thoma

Page 55: A view of Týn Church from Týn Court (Ungelt). Photo © Roman Maleček

Page 56: Týn organ, from the second half of the 17th century, is the oldest preserved organ in Prague. Photo © Zdeněk Thoma

Page 57: left: Gothic stone pulpit from the 15th century. Photo © Zdeněk Thoma

Page 57: right: The Baroque altar Calvary with Gothic carvings by Master of the Týn crucifixion. Photo © Zdeněk Thoma

Page 58: left: A niche in the gable of the central nave. Photo © Zdeněk Thoma

Page 58: right: Altar of John the Baptist with a Renaissance carving of Christ's baptism in the middle. Photo © Zdeněk Thoma

Page 59: The altarpiece of the Assumption of the Virgin Mary by Karel Škréta. Photo © Zdeněk Thoma

Page 60: Church of St Haštal, general view. Photo © Roman Maleček

Page 62 left: Gargoyle under the supporting ribs of the northern two-nave hall. Photo © Jan Rendek

Page 62 right: Statue of the Calvary by the school of F. M. Brokoff. Photo © Zdeněk Thoma

143

Page 63 left: General view into the main nave with the altar and pulpit.
Photo © Zdeněk Thoma

Page 63 right: Close up of the Calvary statue by the school of F. M. Brokoff.
Photo © Zdeněk Thoma

Page 64: Church of St Havel, general view.
Photo © Roman Maleček

Page 66 left: Close up of a Crying St. Mary Magdalena from the Calvary Chapel in St Havel's church. Photo © Zdeněk Thoma

Page 66 right: Close up of the gate of St Havel's church. Photo © Zdeněk Thoma

Page 67: Statues of the Calvary by F. M. Brokoff.
Photo © Zdeněk Thoma

Page 68: Statues of saints on the main façade by F. M. Jäckel from early 18th Century.
Photo © Roman Maleček

Page 69: Calvary chapel in the St Havel's church.
Photo © Zdeněk Thoma

Page 70: Bethlehem chapel, general view.
Photo © Zdeněk Thoma

Page 72: Mural musical notations from the Jistebniz Hymn Book. Photo © Zdeněk Thoma

Page 73 left: Neo-Gothic windows and a well.
Photo © Zdeněk Thoma

Page 73 right: Renewed pulpit and the original stone jambs of doors and windows.
Photo © Jan Rendek

Page 74: Church of Martin in the Wall, view from the Coal market. Photo © Roman Maleček

Page 76 left: Church of Martin in the Wall, view of the apsid. Photo © Roman Maleček

Page 76 right: View of the interior from the pulpit and communion table. Photo © Roman Maleček

Page 77: Stone gargoyle.
Photo © Roman Maleček

Page 78: Church of St Jiljí, general view.
Photo © Zdeněk Thoma

Page 80: View of the main altar and side altar of St. Thomas Aquinas. Photo © Zdeněk Thoma

Page 81: Altar of Our Lady of the Rosary.
Photo © Zdeněk Thoma

Page 82 left: One of four Rococo confessionals.
Photo © Zdeněk Thoma

Page 82 right: Close up of the main altar.
Photo © Zdeněk Thoma

Page 83 left: Ceiling fresco of the north aisle.
Photo © Zdeněk Thoma

Page 83 right: A ceiling fresco depicting the preaching of St. Dominic and St. Francis to the heretics by V. V. Rainer. Photo © Zdeněk Thoma

Page 84: Close up of the ceiling fresco of St. Dominic and St. Francis preaching to the heretics. Photo © Zdeněk Thoma

Page 85: Carving on one of the four Rococo confessionals. Photo © Zdeněk Thoma

Page 86: View of the church of Our Lady of the Snow from Franciscan Gardens.
Photo © Roman Maleček

Page 88: Aerial view of the Church of Our Lady of the Snow and the Franciscan Garden.
Photo © Jan Rendek

Page 89 top: View of the presbytery.
Photo © Roman Maleček

Page 89 bottom: Looting of the Church of Our Lady of the Snow on the 15th of February 1611 on a copperplate engraving by J. Baptista Collaerts. AMP 1702

Page 90: The Church of St. Jindřich and Kunhuta, general view from the tower Jindřišská.
Photo © Roman Maleček

Page 92 left: Looking towards the tower of St Jindřich which juts out on the left behind the temple tower on the left.
Photo © Roman Maleček

Page 92 right: View of the main nave towards the altar. Photo © Jan Rendek

Page 93: View of the presbytery.
Photo © Jan Rendek

Page 94: Church of the Holy Ghost, general view.
Photo © Roman Maleček

Page 96 left: Church of the Holy Ghost with the Spanish Synagogue. Photo © Roman Maleček

Page 96 right: Church of the Holy Ghost, view of the main nave. Photo © Roman Maleček

Page 97: Church of the Holy Ghost, late Baroque altar from around 1740.
Photo © Roman Maleček

Page 98 left: Francis Xavier preaches unto the Gentiles, relief on the gate of the altar.
Photo © Roman Maleček

Page 98 right: Gothic Pieta from around 1400.
Photo © Roman Maleček

Page 99 left: Church of the Holy Ghost, pulpit.
Photo © Roman Maleček

Page 99 right: Organ from the 19th century.
Photo © Roman Maleček

Page 100: The Church of St. Peter and Peter's Tower, view from Petrská street.
Photo © Roman Maleček

Page 102: Close up of a Baroque pulpit with reliefs. Photo © Roman Maleček

Page 103: The main altar of St. Peter with a painting depicting Christ handing the keys to St Peter. Photo © Zdeněk Thoma

Page 104 left: Crucifix to the left of the main entrance. Photo © Zdeněk Thoma

Page 104 right: Evening view of St. Peter and Peter's tower. Photo © Zdeněk Thoma

Page 105: Baroque statue of St.John of Nepomuk from the mid-18th century on the south wall of the presbytery. Photo © Zdeněk Thoma

Page 106: Church of St Peter, organ.
Photo © Zdeněk Thoma

Page 107: Close up of the main altar from the year 1740. Photo © Zdeněk Thoma

Page 108: Church of St Stephen, general view.
Photo © Roman Maleček

Page 110 left: Gothic stone pulpit.
Photo © Zdeněk Thoma

Page 110 right: The altarpiece the Stoning of St. Stephen from the 17th century by M. Zimprecht.
Photo © Zdeněk Thoma

Page 111: View of the main nave in the direction of the altar. Photo © Zdeněk Thoma

Page 112: St Longin's rotunda.
Photo © Roman Maleček

Page 114: St Longin's rotunda.
Photo © Roman Maleček

Page 115: St. Longin's Rotunda with the Church of St. Steven. Photo © Zdeněk Thoma

Page 116: Church of St Cyril and Methodius, general view. Photo © Jan Rendek

Page 118 left: View of the main nave with icons.
Photo © Roman Maleček

Page 118 right: Picture of St. Wenceslaus and St Ludmila. Photo © Roman Maleček

Page 119: The crypt. Photo © Roman Maleček

Page 120: Church of the Most Sacred Heart of our Lord, general view. Photo © Zdeněk Thoma

Page 122 left: Aerial view of George of Poděbrad Square with the Church of the Sacred Heart.
Photo © Jan Rendek

Page 122 right: Church of the Most Sacred Heart of our Lord, general view.
Photo © Zdeněk Thoma

Page 123: Church of the Most Sacred Heart of our Lord, view of the interior.
Photo © Zdeněk Thoma

Page 124: Old New Synagogue, general view from Maisel street. Photo © Zdeněk Thoma

Page 126: Old New Synagogue and the original Jewish Town Hall. Photo © Roman Maleček

Page 127 left: Old New Synagogue, view of the interior - bima with a Gothic grille.
Photo © Zdeněk Thoma

Page 127 right: Rostrum and the Tabernacle.
Photo © Zdeněk Thoma

Page 128: Spanisch synagogue, façade with typical elements of Moorish architecture.
Photo © Zdeněk Thoma

Page 130 left: Spanish synagogue, main hall, view to the east wall with the sanctuary.
Photo © Zdeněk Thoma

Page 130 right: Organ in the Spanish synagogue.
Photo © Zdeněk Thoma

Page 131: The eastern wall with the sanctuary (aron ha-kodesh). Photo © Zdeněk Thoma

Page 132: Maisel synagogue, general view.
Photo © Roman Maleček

Page 135: Maisel synagogue, Neo-Gothic facade with slabs of the ten Commandments.
Photo © Zdeněk Thoma

Page 141: Church of St Nicholas in the Lesser Town. Photo © Roman Maleček